Prayers on the Road Home

Prayers on the Road Home

Benjamin Martin

ISBN-13: 978-1976118982
ISBN-10: 1976118980

To my beloved,
life-long companion, Teri.

From our sacred conversations,
these conversations with Spirit.

For the grace-filled hours given us
and for Teri's careful shaping of these words,
I am ever grateful.

Order of Prayers

Introduction

The prayers in this collection have inhabited and in-formed me throughout the last three decades of the jam-packed, the amazing, the difficult, the tumultuous moments of life. These prayers seem to have come by way of my fingers revealing themselves only when I would begin to write. Though they emerged from me, it was always a surprise to discover their final expression.

For many years, it has been my privilege to be part of an interfaith spiritual community called Christuman. One of my contributions has been to provide a prayer for each gathering at the sacred table and many of those prayers are included here. I have organized the collection around the themes that we celebrate according to our liturgical calendar: the mysteries of Enlightenment, Grace and Love, Death and Resurrection, Creativity, Joy, the I am, the Yang, the Yin, the Quest, God, Thanksgiving and Home, Birth and Rebirth.

With a fulltime job in the tech world and a busy family life, my days were frequently overbooked. Often I found myself hatching a prayer quite literally "on the road home" from work, or last minute on my way to a service. Disconcerting to all who knew my secret, I would have pen and pad ready in the car to take advantage of any "stop" aspect of the "stop-and-go traffic" pulling in the words and putting to paper a prayer that expressed the challenges of the day.

It is my hope that these prayers can serve as a companion for you on your road home and help foster your conversation with the Sacred as you meet the challenges and day-to-day activities of your life.

Benjamin Martin

Prayer of the Prayer in Me

O Beloved Spirit,
I have a prayer in me but it has no words.
I have a prayer in me but the thoughts it needs
to give it form do not line up in a straight grammatical line.
I have a prayer in me but it is not attached to
a wish or a want or a desire.
I have a prayer in me that I don't recognize as my own.
Instead, I think this prayer is You giving groanings to
who I am and could be and can be.

I have a prayer in me that I think is somehow foreign
to the me I grew up to be,
but native to the me I have always been.
And this prayer says, "Breathe me in and breathe me out
for I am the holy breath and I take you in and I take you out."
It is not a prayer I recognize as mine,
but it is one that would claim me as its own.

I have a prayer in me
not attached to a wish or a want or a desire—
a prayer that came in through inspiration
and found its voice along the cords of my own soundings.
I have a prayer in me that must come through me
and back out of me but still it is You interceding through me.
It is my way of becoming You, and You becoming my breath,
both in and out and through and around.

I have a prayer in me. Let me not cut short its breath
until its holiness is wholly me,
and I am the prayer of the prayer in me.

Amen

Enlightenment

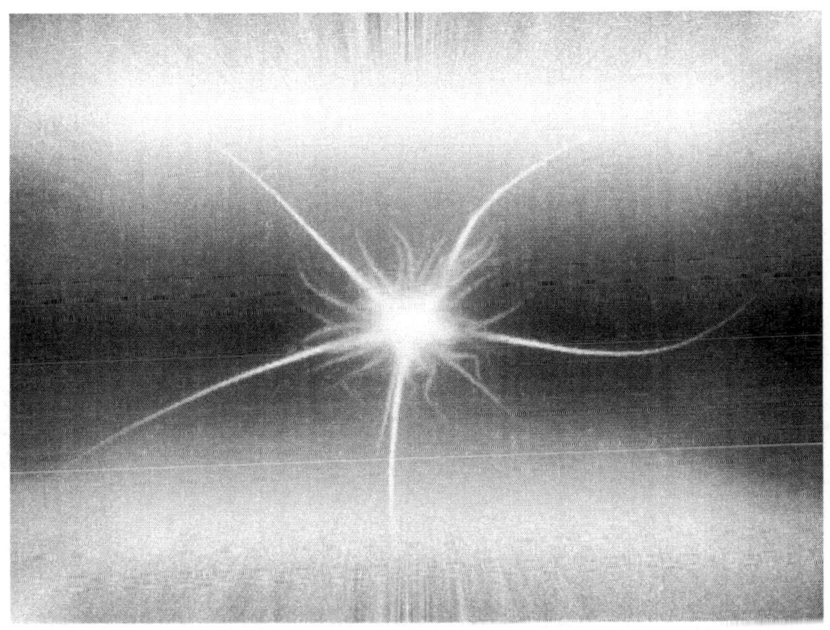

A man must himself be cleansed before cleansing others;
become wise that he may make others wise;
become light, before he can give light;
draw near to God before he can bring others near;
be hallowed, before he can hallow them;
be possessed of hands before leading others by the hand;
and of wisdom, before he can speak wisely.

Gregory of Nyssa

Prayer for Light

O Beloved Spirit,
Anoint me with Your light,
that what cannot be seen
will be clarified in what is awakened.

Anoint me with Your light,
not so I will find more,
but that more of what is ancient
may be revealed within me.

Anoint me with Your light,
that the gray pixels of matter
may give way to the fire of Your spirit.

Anoint me with Your light,
that I might ignite into all that is becoming—
not afraid to look upon my ashes
nor to be singular in my Oneness.

You are my light and my spark.
Anoint the essential
that I might give back in its fullness
what You have fully given.

Amen

Prayer of Spirals

O Beloved Spirit,
We move in spirals, as we return to the beginning
of a year we declare "new."
We move in spirals as we chart our course
by the star we declare our "one chance."
We move in spirals as we look at the "where-we-were"
and wonder at the "where-we-will-be."
And in this moment, a sense of sameness
that this moment is like so many moments before.
And in this moment, a sense of newness
that this moment is like no other.
And in this Here, the spiral of life
with so much to embrace.
And in this Here, the spiral of death
with so much to release.
Here—no other place more sacred.
Here—no other chance more ripe.
Here—no other embrace more vital.

Let us bring our gifts to the star
that captured our imaginations so long ago—
the star that is etched on our foreheads,
the star that shines out over a sacred birth.
Let us bring our gifts to the star
in honor of the life we have been given to live,
in honor of the death we have been given to die,
in honor of the divine lineage
embedded in the trough of this body.
Let us bring our gifts to the star
that the transcendent light can be made immanent within us.
Amen

Prayer for Clear Looking

O Beloved Spirit,
We are in a deep sleep on a dark night.
If ever we knew—now, no memory.
If ever we saw—now, no vision.
We scan the skies but see no sign to arouse us.
And so, we look to those who saw before us
and through their seeing, we see "wise."

How wise the Magi who not only saw a star,
but, unlike all others,
recognized that it could lead them.
How wise the Magi who not only heard of the birth,
but, unlike all others,
were readied for the journey.

And so it is, that seeing the Magi we see
that until the star be in us,
we cannot recognize it,
until the birth becomes us,
we cannot find its place.

May we be diligent in our search for the star
and wise in our way to the birth,
that through the clarity of our looking
we may magnify and magnify again
the epiphany of Your grace.

Amen

Prayer from a Winter Place

O Beloved Spirit,
Find me where I am,
in my dark time and in my winter place.
Amid my cries of not knowing,
open me to wise gifts:
Your gold, a reminder of royal lineage;
Your frankincense, a cleansing essence for renewal;
Your myrrh, a sustainer of soul
through all the deaths I need to die.

Find me where I am,
in my dark time and in my winter place.
Despite my cries of "If only"
and my excuses of "I'm not ready"
and my indignant protests of
"These gifts are not enough."

Find me where I am,
in spite of where I think I've been
or where I wish to be.

Find me where I am,
so that where I go, I go with
Your gold, a sense of my heritage—
Your frankincense, a sense of renewal in all that I do—
Your myrrh, a sense of the sacred through many deaths.
Amen

Prayer to Stay Clear of the Small

O Beloved Spirit,
There are days when the air is not so clear,
and the view is clouded by smallness;
when the focus is fragmented
and particulates of debris collect
like a haze in the mind.
In the denseness of the small,
how do I stay clear of the small?
In the thick haze of the small,
how do I stay clean of the small?

Be my breath,
that I might clear my mind with light.
Be my breath,
that I might purify my heart with light.

Light fill me.
Breath fill me.
That though I am in the smallness,
I be not of the smallness.
Though I am bounded by smallness,
I be not constricted into smallness.

Be my breath, O Beloved Spirit,
my inspiration of light.

Amen

Prayer to Be Mindful of Soul

O Beloved Spirit,
When our discontent clouds our vision,
how do we sort between the petty and the core,
between the surface hurt and the deeper scar,
between the painful symptom and the origin of our pain?
When our discontent colors our outlook, how do we see
beyond the immediate to find the underlying,
beyond the temporary to find the causal,
beyond the band-aid to find the healing?

At times, we lose our way in the turbulence
and cannot align our sights;
we deplete our energy on the small
and cannot clarify that which is focal to the soul.
Remind us of the blessed poverty of our spirit
that we might take root in what we lack,
that we might take root in what we do not know,
that we might take root in what we most need.

In our discontent, in our turbulence,
bring us back to our poverty,
that we might see You in all we are and are becoming,
that we might be ever mindful of Soul.

Amen

Prayer for the Return

O Beloved Spirit,
Your liturgy of daytime light,
Your rays of expanding vision with each day
a little earlier, a little wider, a little longer,
we celebrate the Return.
And though only bare beginnings
are buried in the dead of this winter yet therein,
an ember of remembrance that a fresh start,
a seedbed of renewal,
waits beneath the barren surface.

O Beloved Spirit,
May we not ignore
the newness buried in our familiar.
May we not disparage this new day
with a jaded sense of "just another",
that daytime light heralds merely
what we had been expecting all along.
May we not wear out the hope
that birth can occur even now.
May it always and ever reveal to us
the miracle of "anew, yet again".

O Beloved Spirit,
More like a child in our seeing,
more like a song in our expressing,
more like a color in our unfolding—
we celebrate Your liturgy of daytime light
as it envelops the sky with more and more of its fire
and creates and reveals a newness
we had not seen or known was possible.

The epiphany of light is all around us.
May its revelation awaken the new again in us.
Amen

Prayer of Confluence

O Beloved Spirit,
In the confluence of this moment,
in the currents of times past and times future,
in the intercoursing play of remembrances before
and of visions after,
we pull in the current of this prayer
and are moved by the current,
and are made sacred by the current,
and are transformed by the current.
For the confluence of this moment, we are grateful.

In the confluence of this moment,
in the currents of sacred time,
in the interplay of body and mind and soul,
we pull in the current of this prayer
that rushes through our hearts here,
that moves us to gratefulness now,
that upends us with a love most unexpected always.
For the confluence of this moment, we are grateful.

In the confluence of this moment,
in the currents of genius
unfolding through music and art,
through poetry and dance,
through right action and courage,
we pull in the current of this prayer
that rides through us in joy.
For the marvel of being human
that currents through us in ecstasy,
for the marvel of becoming human
that currents through us in *enthusiasmos*,
for the awakening of Spirit within,
and the awakening Spirit without,
for the confluence of this moment, we are grateful.

O Beloved Spirit, the current in our Current,
we sing You and pray that You will sing through us.
For the confluence of this moment, we are grateful.
Amen

Prayer of Epiphany

O Beloved Spirit,
We scan the skies for the star that will deliver us.
Some days it seems like such a stalled labor
as we move among so many encumbrances—
each day's worries, anxieties, doubts;
so many days, we are unsure of our footing
and uncertain of our standing.

We scan the skies for the star that will deliver us.
Some days it seems like the full bloom is fast approaching,
and we have such little time to be present, to be awake—
each day forwards us through the necessary and the important
leaving us with more to do than we were able to get done
and our wishes and our goals and our dreams pile up.

We scan the skies for the star that will deliver us.
Though we are learning to detach from the outcomes,
let us not disconnect from the vital.
Though we are learning to move to our death with grace,
let us not forget to live with grace.
Though we are learning to become more of who we are,
let us not stray from the Being that is in this moment.

O Beloved Spirit, it is true that we are an epiphany of the divine.
Let us hold to the star in us, this one chance to be.
It is true that we are an epiphany of the infinite.
Let us hold to the eternal through the Love that transforms us.
It is true that we are an epiphany,
a unique revelation of the omnipresent God.
Let us embrace the divine appearances
manifested in those around us
as well as the divine appearances manifested within us.

We scan the skies for the star that will deliver us
and know it to be no further than in the inverting and everting
of the epiphany of our being, of our becoming Human.
Amen

Prayer for Salvation

O Beloved Spirit,
We wonder about salvation.
It seems so old-fashioned to us,
forged in sermons of fire and brimstone;
and yet, we wonder.
It is not fear of hell that gives us pause,
but fear of squandering our one chance to be.
It is not our conviction of an unworthiness,
but fear of settling for less than our greatest possibility.
It is not our sense of guilt or shame,
but fear of the lukewarm, the tepid, the mediocre.

O Beloved Spirit, where is our salvation?
A digital dance of necessity and desire upends us.
We find ourselves distracted in a wilderness of the small.
O Beloved Spirit, where is our salvation?
Held captive by the shadows
that flicker against cave walls—
our flat panels, our smart-screens.
O Beloved Spirit, where is our salvation,
the means to unmediated light?

Immerse us in clear, clarifying waters
that we may be raised from the death we are living,
that we may herald the only-begotten nature of our essence—
our essential, our most important, our very own soul.
Immerse us in clear, purifying waters
that we may lay claim to our only-begotten *potentia*—
our unique *origo*, our one chance to shine,
our one chance to see and be seen.
Immerse us in clear, clarifying waters,
that we might be raised in a newness of life.
O Beloved Spirit, bring us to salvation,
a full-realization of our only-begottenness.

Amen

Prayer for Presence of Spirit

O Beloved Spirit,
Our spirits have been fished out of the Before
and given minds and hearts and creative energy
with which to rule Now until released into the Hereafter.

Give us the presence of Your spirit
to rule from the mind
with an infusion of compassion.

Give us the presence of Your spirit
to rule from the heart
with an infusion of contemplation.

Give us the presence of Your spirit
to rule from the creative energy
with an infusion of inspiration.

That with this presence of Holy Spirit
we may continue to sustain the
potential of the human to continue to become Human.

We are ever grateful for the presence of Your spirit
in the life of our lives.

Amen

Prayer within Prayer

O Beloved Spirit,
We pray this prayer in full understanding
of how little we understand prayer.
And as this prayer courses through us,
we wonder at the irony of these words
giving grammar to the unspeakable
and giving sequence to what does not necessarily follow.
Too funny, too true, too holy to be imprisoned in a string of words
and yet, this prayer to us is like wings to a bird.
We do not know what else to do but be led by this prayer,
and let this prayer have its way with us.

We pray this prayer in full understanding
of how little we understand prayer.
and though we know we are doomed from the beginning,
we are startled by an urge to pray,
to give voice to the ineffable joy of being alive,
of being graced by a Spirit that is so holy,
so immense, so deep that we are immersed
in a love that surpasses all our understanding.

We pray this prayer in full understanding
of how little we understand prayer.
But we trust that this prayer
planted in our hearts from the beginning
will lead us beyond all understanding
and bear the empathic groanings
and longings of our innermost ground.
We trust this prayer with its infolding and its unfolding,
with its inverting and its everting.
May it find clear passage through us.
May we become as one voice
with the prayer that prays through us.

Amen

Grace and Love

Holy Spirit,
giving life to all life, moving all creatures,
root of all things, washing them clean,
wiping out their mistakes, healing their wounds,
You are our true life, luminous, wonderful,
awakening the heart from its ancient sleep.

Hildegard of Bingen

Prayer of a Grace-filled Life

O Beloved Spirit,
Each moment of love—
the delightful surprise of a shared joke,
the compassionate exchange in response to a hurt,
the embrace of a knowing recognition.

Each moment of learning—
the ah-ha of the insight,
the ecstasy of hearing it as if for the first time,
the connections made from such disparate sources.

Each moment of seeing—
the snow-flocked trees offset by the blazing blue sky,
the dark, viscous night filled with stars from ages past,
the recognition of the unseen at work in everyday choices.

Each moment of the generative life—
the fruitful, the bountiful, the amazing, the miraculous,
the loud enunciation of the impossible–
echoing through the very foundations of our lives.

We swim in a sea of grace
and are infused with a Spirit of love.
Let us accept this grace-filled life.
Let us accept this love-infused universe.
Let us embrace this ceaseless generosity
and let us burn ever so brightly
through this moment of love,
this moment of learning,
this moment of seeing,
this moment of the generative life.

Amen

Prayer for the Grace to Pray

O Beloved Spirit,
There are times when we feel our pores close up
and our minds shut down
and our hearts fill with frustration
and we do not want to pray.
And that is when we know, we must pray.

There are times when the events of the day
seem but chores
and there is no dignity left,
no grace to be found.
And that is when we know, we must pray.

There are times when all the things that we can't control
converge and seem to thwart the thing we can control.
And we shut down the intercession of our hearts and thoughts
and will not let them flow.
And that is when we know, we must open ourselves to pray.

And so we pray—
not for rescue, intervention or solution—
but for the grace to pray the prayer we do not want to pray—
for the grace to reopen our pores
and circulate the love that is already, always there.
Amen

Prayer of Vigil

O Beloved Spirit,
We join in vigil for those
who must midwife the death of one they love.
The labor pains have started.
They come in waves
of tiredness, of pain, of wanting to let go,
of memories past and of goodbyes.

No one can do it for us;
we each make the crossing alone.
All we can do is surround the dying
and those who tend to the dying
with the light of our vigilant love.

Together, we focus the scattered dance
of our thoughts and activities
into a confluence of empathic hope and love—
a nourishing vigil
that feeds the soul of the one who is dying,
that feeds the souls of those who serve.

For the family of our loved one,
we keep watch with them
and send them our sustaining love and prayers.

To the one who is dying,
we extend our compassion
and pray for a beautiful death
befitting the beautiful life this one has lived.

O Beloved Spirit, send our love to these.

Amen

Prayer in Thanksgiving for Grace

O Beloved Spirit,
While we wear a body
and nourish it with food,
it is Your grace that sustains
our being and our becoming.
Your grace which gives us life
that then renews it,
Your grace which brings us tears
that then yields compassion,
Your grace which connects the fragmented
that then initiates new vision.

Our life, our tears, our fragments
are but the media through which Your grace infuses.
Prepare in us a clean heart
and a clear mind
that we may better receive
the ever-surprising gift of Your grace.

Amen

Prayer for Mercy

O Beloved Spirit,
I am disquieted by the distance incurred
by being once removed:
from conviction because conviction seems so one-sided;
from compassion because compassion seems so vulnerable;
from commitment because commitment seems so confining.

Once removed from community
because community requires so much time and place
and time is chopped up into disconnected segments
and place is scattered across an urban sprawl.

Once removed from participation
because participation requires whole-heartedness
and to do it all requires a more frugal approach.

Once removed from joy
because joy might not bloom when its roots—
conviction, compassion, commitment, community and participation—
are once removed from the very ground in which they grow.

Kyrie eleison. Kyrie eleison. Kyrie eleison.
Have mercy on me.
Help me remove the distance I've created
by being once removed.

Amen

Prayer for Grace

O Beloved Spirit,
In the gap between how we find ourselves
and how we want to be found;
in the gap of how we find others to be
and how we would want them to be;
in the gap of the way things are
and how we would choose them to be;
be love in us, be love through us,
belove us, belove us, belove us.

In the disappointment of how things turned out
instead of how we had envisioned them;
in the disappointment of what we had wanted to accomplish
instead of what we have accomplished so far;
in the disappointment of being disappointed,
instead of the hopefulness we had so hoped for;
be love in us, be love through us,
belove us, belove us, belove us.

It is not a clean and perfected dance in which we find ourselves.
Our steps falter. We fall out of step. We lose the rhythm.
It is not a clean and perfected dance in which we find ourselves.
We don't always hear the strains or recognize the beat.
It is not a clean and perfected dance in which we find ourselves.
We are self-conscious, self-critical, self-awkward;
be love in us, be love through us,
belove us, belove us, belove us.

O Beloved Spirit, we seek grace
in this dance in which we find ourselves:
that we may delight in the surprise of breaking past the impossible,
that we may joy in the movement that takes us out of the expected,
that we may find ecstasy in becoming the music,
if only for a moment,
be grace in us, be grace through us,
be-grace us, be-grace us, be-grace us.

Amen

Prayer for Recognizing Grace

O Beloved Spirit,
No green pastures this day,
but down-turned winds
inflected with grit and gravel.

No quiet waters this day,
but churned-up rapids
with a wild backwash of river.

No undisturbed sun this day,
but an onrush of clouds
ponderous with threats of more threats.

No pastoral contemplation
in this mix of disquiet.

And yet, in the wind—seed,
in the rapids—rich soil,
in the clouds—rain.

May we not discount the grace
embedded even in this
our longest, darkest of days.

Hold us in Your heart
that we may hold You in ours.

Amen

Prayer Through a Love Song

O Beloved Spirit,
Along the cords of the voice, a vibratory expression of our love;
a song sung in rhythm nuanced with the rich colors of our joy.
We join uniquely as each in the choral crescendo of One;
one voice, one harmony, one song.
And in the marvel of being alive,
being warmed by a star by day
and dazzled by galaxies and universes by night
and fed and nourished by a rich harvest of Your light,
here in this prayer, hear in our prayer,
an inexpressible song of love and delight.

O Beloved Spirit, no note, no lyric,
no sounding from the inner chord of our chord
can intone the depth, the pitch, the reach of the beloving
that draws us closer into the unfathomable mystery of Your love
alive in us, and us alive in and through You.
O Beauty that awakens our senses with essences so unmistakable—
of mint and cloves and chocolate and cinnamon,
and fills our eyes with the green of sage and pine,
spruce and tall grasses,
and touches us with surfaces of stone and wood and plant and fur
and upends us with sounds of jays and crows,
chickadees and squirrels,
and delights us with tastes of curry and milk and peach and honey
and engages our hearts as we learn to be and become
belover and beloved.

O Beloved Spirit, no note, no lyric,
no sounding from the inner chord of our chord
can intone the depth, the pitch, the reach of the beloving
that enfolds us in this mystery dance of life.

Here in this prayer, hear in our prayer,
an inexpressible song of love and delight.
We adore thee. We adore thee. We adore thee.
Amen

Prayer of Kyrie Eleison

O Beloved Spirit,
While we think we understand pain,
it is not until we are stung once more by its sting
that we know again: *kyrie eleison.*

While we think we understand grief,
it is not until we are weighed down once more by its weight
that we know again: *kyrie eleison.*

While we think we understand death,
it is not until we are stopped short by the shortness
of the life we once knew,
that we know again: *kyrie eleison.*

While it is our wish to be spared the pain,
we know but one prayer: *kyrie eleison.*
While it is our wish to be spared the grief,
we know but one prayer: *kyrie eleison.*
While it is our wish to be spared from death,
we know but one prayer: *kyrie eleison.*

Have mercy on us: *kyrie eleison.*
Hear our prayer: *kyrie eleison.*

Amen

Prayer to Be Heard

O Beloved Spirit,
Our hearts are made tender with the unexpected,
with outcomes we didn't realize.
Out of our unknowing, hear us.

Our hearts are made tender with the unexpected,
with regrets we can't make right.
Out of our darkness, hear us.

Our hearts are made tender with the unexpected,
with the unspoken we can't speak.
Out of our loneliness, hear us.

Our hearts are made tender with the unexpected,
with the things we can't fix.
Out of our pain, hear us.

Amen

Prayer for the Infilling of the Moment

O Beloved Spirit,
Too often, we lose awareness of the breath that inspires us.
Too often, we lose awareness of the breath that stirs us.
Too often, we lose awareness of the breath that sings us.
Caught in the next and the next and the next,
we lose our connection to the infilling of this moment here,
the infilling of this moment now,
with the infilling of Your vital breath always.

What a chance we have to play and be played.
What a chance we have to take in and be taken in.
What a chance we have to renew and be renewed.
Even Here, in the next and the next and the next,
in the infilling of this moment here,
in the infilling of this moment now,
in the infilling of Your vital breath always.

Too often, we forget the quickening of this spirit into body.
Too often, we forget the birth into Now, pushing us into aliveness.
Too often, we forget the inception of Breath that charges us with joy.
Even Here, in the next and the next and the next,
in the infilling of this moment here,
in the infilling of this moment now,
in the infilling of Your vital breath always.

What grace is embedded in these paths of beauty!
What grace is embedded in these paths of sacred heart!
What grace is embedded in these paths of sound and color!
Even Here, in the next and the next and the next—
in the evening rains and morning freshness,
in the sounds of children laughing, teasing, loving,
in the handshakes and hugs—friends and family made holy.

Even Here, in the next and the next and the next,
our infilling of this moment here, our infilling of this moment now,
our infilling of Your vital breath always.

Amen

Prayer for the Joyous Dance of Grace

O Beloved Spirit,
Not in the fulfilling of our dreams
but in the unexpected ways You infill our lives.
Not in the receiving of gifts we have asked for
but in the awakening to gifts we didn't know were already there.
Not in the perfecting of our personalities
but in the nuanced way You belove us, behold us.
Not in the removal of our pain or our disappointments
but in their harvest—empathy, gratefulness, connectedness.

This dance of grace, this grace-full dance unfolds through us
unexpectedly moving through our pain with joy;
through our hardships with insight,
through our regrets with compassion.
This dance of grace, this grace-full dance unfolds
through us unexpectedly finding
joy where we thought to find discouragement,
understanding where we thought to find blockage,
humor where we thought to find mortification.
This dance of grace, this grace-full dance unfolds through us
unexpectedly refreshing:
where we expected only the tired, we find the rejuvenated,
where we expected only the jaded, we find the galvanized,
where we expected only the predetermined, we find the surprising.

Not in fulfilling our dreams
but in exceeding our wildest imaginations:
a cloudburst, a bloom, a sunset, a star-laden galaxy.
Not in receiving desired gifts
but in awakening to gifts beyond measure:
rollicking streams, wind-whispering trees,
the tireless breathing of oceans upon our shores.
Not in perfecting our personalities
but in transformational moments:
changing us, upending us, moving us to friendship and love.
Not in the removal of our pain or our disappointments
but in the glorious offset of Your grace:
restoring us, refinishing us, refining us, refreshing us.
For this joyous dance of grace, we are grateful.

Amen

Death and Resurrection

With thy rude ploughshare, Death, turn up the sod,
And spread the furrow for the seed we sow;
This is the field and Acre of our God,
This is the place where human harvests grow!

Henry Wadsworth Longfellow

Prayer for Pure Vision

O Beloved Spirit,
Here on my bench in a circle of trees,
the soft shimmy of the wind rushes
through the feathery pines of the forest
and stirs awake a bed of needles and the spent brown grasses.
The birds wing in breaking open the day with their staccato trill
and the woodpecker, back at it, beaks the bark in rapid fire
while crows collect overhead intruding with their strident calls.
Ahhh…the sound of return and refreshment

And in this new beginning,
a nod, a grateful blessing to the old, to the dead,
to the interiority of the dark and cold
to the warmth of the hearth and fire.
I inhale the solitariness of winter
and exhale it in a sigh of relief
releasing the grip of the old.
Ahhh…the sound of return and refreshment.

O Beloved Spirit, a great onrush of life,
a great exhalation of spirit, a great furrow of light
overturns my days and exposes my earth
to the joy, to the thrill, to the anticipation of
what is just beginning to begin—Spring.
Ahhh…the sound of return and refreshment.

Ahhh, this grand moment gifted us
by the pipping of light
opening buds of life, sprouting seeds into plants,
cracking open this shell of mine.
Let me embrace the birth.
Let me awaken to the taste and sight and smell of Spring
and feel the reverent call in the wind
to live out my days renewed,
to fulfill my calling to create,
to become a new creation.
Ahhh…the sound of return and refreshment.

Amen

Prayer to the Reawakened

O Beloved Spirit,
As if we have been in a great sleep
entombed within the too much of our days
as if we have been in hibernation,
we yearn for an awakening
for a generative joy of re-creation and recreation,
for a breakout into light and song.

O Beloved Spirit,
As if we have been in a great sleep
entombed into the too much of our days
as if we have been in hibernation,
we yearn to release the death in our bones,
to embrace life,
to rise up from the slab of unawareness,
to roll away the stone.

O Beloved Spirit,
As if we have been in a great sleep
entombed into the too much of our days,
as if we have been in hibernation,
we yearn for renewal,
for a wider aperture of wonder,
for an unconstricted path of beloving,
for a renewed opening of heart.

Death to our sleep!
Death to our entombment!
Death to our hibernation!
Let us renew and be renewed,
embrace and be embraced,
know and be known.
Let us roll away the stone
into the marvel of a new awakening.

Amen

Prayer to a Good Day to Die Again

O Beloved Spirit,
We weary of unclenching the very things that have us in their grip.
We weary of the letting go that comes in unhitching
ourselves from what we hold to be so dear.
We weary of the seeming unfairness that comes in detaching
ourselves from the very thing we take pride in.
Must it be?

And yet, if it must be, perhaps this day is a good day to die—
the freshness of the dawn brightened by the light of Venus,
the newness of the ground potent with hidden seed taking root,
the crispness of Spring bursting into a thousand thousand buds.
Ah yes, if it must be, perhaps this day is a good day to die—
a day to learn to birth the death that comes to term in us—
a day to learn to embrace what is most holy in this Here—
a day to learn to forgive so that the giving can be restored.
Ah yes, if it must be, perhaps this day is a good day to die—
for letting go of the image we have enshrined
with tenacious self-esteem—
for letting go of the disappointment
we have so rehearsed and kept in play—
for letting go of the anger we have nurtured
so as to not lose its fiery burn.
If it must be—and it must be—this is a good day to die.

Ah, but this day is a good day to die, O Spirit most holy—
who continues to infill the clearings, to infuse the openings—
who continues to restore the wounds with compassion,
Make fresh the depleted, make new the jaded.
It must be. It must be.
O Beloved Spirit, do not let us lose sight
of how vital to life this death we are called to die.
Yes, it must be that You winnow the least of us.
Yes, it must be—so as to uncover the best of us.
Yes, it must be—so we become at one with all that is human
and with all that is divine.

Amen

Prayer to Remain Here and Keep Watch

O Beloved Spirit,
Though not yet full term,
we are seeded with a death we are to birth.
Conceived in us like a baby, it waits until its time
and then delivers us from what we have come to know
as we deliver it into what we cannot know.
This secret knowledge of our death
is a potent boost to our life as it quickens our joy
and fills us with an urgent sense of the shortness of our breath,
the compactness of our journey,
the one chance we have to love and be loved.
This secret knowledge teaches us
an ecstasy in a night bath of stars,
a delight in the daylight of friendship,
an elation in the holding and in the beholding
of the miracle of still being alive.

And there are those we know for whom the point of death is near.
And for them, we are called to remain Here—
to be Here—to just be Here—and to keep watch with them.
As they enter into their prayer of Gethsemane,
supply us the grace, the graciousness needed to remain Here.
Supply us the presence of mind to keep watch,
to be a source of solace and strength,
to hold them in prayer as they pray.
May we not default on our calling,
succumb to a sleep of denial and avoidance,
retreat for fear of intruding.
Rather, supply us the grace, the graciousness needed
to remain Here and keep watch.

Though not yet full term,
we are seeded with a death we are to birth.
May we ready ourselves for this blooming.
And though we know not the date we are due
may we carry our death's mounting force with dignity
living to our fullest this one-chance impossibility.
Supply us the grace, the graciousness needed
to remain Here and to keep watch.

Amen

Prayer for the Times of Between

O Beloved Spirit,
It is a time of between.
Buried in my busyness,
I am somewhere after a closing
and somewhere before an opening.
My readiness seems so long in coming,
my beforeness so long in having been.
While I've let go of what I once wished for,
I seem so far from what I am moving toward.

It is a time of between.
After the death but before the Easter,
after the Easter but before the ascension,
after the ascension but before the Pentecost,
I wander in the wilderness Between.

It is a time of between—
between what I know I don't want
and knowing how to know what I need;
between recognizing what was holding me back
and grasping what will send me forward;
between no longer wanting greatness in their eyes
and seeing with the eyes of my own greatness.

In these times of between, teach me to persevere
though the days seem tedious and my efforts without effect.
Teach me to persevere,
that I will not weary of the beloving
even when without the believing.

Amen

Prayer for Easter of Our Christ

O Beloved Spirit,
In our concern for feeding the hungry,
have we lost sight of nourishing the soul?
In our concern for justice for all,
have we lost sight of restoring the One in each?
In our concern for an equal share of goods for everyone,
have we lost sight of the treasure within the each?
Re-vision this loss of sight. Raise us up anew.

In our efforts to better organize our time,
have we lost sight of the timeless, the eternal?
In our efforts to do it all without flaw,
have we lost sight of the small voice of no thing, of nothing?
In our efforts to know more and understand all,
have we lost sight of unknowing what cannot be known
and of un-controlling what cannot be controlled?
Re-vision this loss of sight. Raise us up anew.

As we compensate for the inequities around us
and the inadequacies within us,
we fall prey to our idea of a global goodness
and lose touch with the personal.
Save us from our goodness
that we may experience renewal through our Godness.

Bless this quiet celebration of the Easter in our all.
Bless gatherings of friends
that they may honor the Easter in the Each.
Re-vision our loss of sight.
Renew our hope in the personal.
Realign us to the One.
Let us reverence the Easter of the Christ
through the Easter of our Christ.

Amen

Prayer for the Thaw

O Beloved Spirit,
It has been a long thaw this season with
blooms reluctant, leaves late to the dance
and the green of the hillside slow to surface.
Unsettling skies have delivered blustery winds
and winter more than spring seems sown
into the dark afternoon clouds.
Why so long this grip,
when we were so ready to be ready?
What is it about the impending season
that is taking so long to prepare?
Yet, while we weary of winter,
we hope to weather our weariness
and to awaken to a stirring, a renewed hunger,
a resilience of beloving.

It has been a long thaw this season.
At times—still burrowed,
buried beneath the too-muchness
of the burdening news of the day.
We are long in thawing; in breaking forth into greens,
into the color of bulbs unfurled,
into the blooming burst of yellows and purples and reds.

Breathe us, O Beloved Spirit,
inspire into the ground of us, a breath of Spring;
inspire into the earth of us, a breath of Ahhh;
inspire into the heart of us, a renewed awakening
to the marvelous mystery of being alive—
the universe's one chance to be awake in our human.
Amen

Prayer for Renewal

O Beloved Spirit,
We call upon the life in us
to regenerate new life—
to replace those cells no longer vital
and to revitalize our hearts, our minds, our dedication.
We live in such a jumble of shoulds and rights and wants.
It seems we cannot sustain a rhythm of hours, of seasons, of prayer.
Renew us.

Make our eyes new.
Fire our love that it may flow strong and rich.
Take the death in us and from its ashes
grow green visions and deep-down *imaginatio*.
May our *arête* germinate new action;
our contemplative time, new insight.
Turn our disappointments into joy,
our frustrations into hope.
For this season of renewal, we are grateful.
May this season be reborn in us.

Amen

Prayer of Spring

O Beloved Spirit,
It is with delight we greet the change in seasons
and all the flourish of Spring:
the green of grass, the color of early buds,
the extension of light on both ends of the day.
It is with delight we greet the change in our lives
as we ride the wave of the unexpected,
in and out of new things and the death of old ones.
It is with delight we discover things we did not know
and stake out things we still have yet to understand.
It is with delight that we unfold in a world of surprises
made up of and by the Creator Spirit,
the creative Creator that courses through our days and nights.
It is with delight that we uncover the power of transformation
and the ability to be reborn.

This is our season of resurrection
when the dormant is reawakened,
and death is cleared away for new sprouts.
The son of the Creator is re-membered on a cross
and then raised from the grave where the stone was rolled away.
In this season of Easter
let us celebrate it by becoming Easter.
May the lineage of the Divine be reborn in us.
May we share in the delight of the surprise—
the miracles of rebirth, the hope of the unexpected.
Amen

Prayer for Regeneration

O Beloved Spirit,
The time changes. The sunlight extends
and we see more of the day—
earlier and later.
What was dead, only dormant,
buds into hints of color.
Where there was but a hard surface,
now new sprouts; ground newly broken.

The last season—cold and fogged skies—
we watched as a loved one's memory
slipped into unrightable tangles
and we learned how much of who we are
is in the connections we make:
the contact with eyes,
the recognition of heart,
the link from the days gone by
with the link to the hopes for tomorrow.

In this season of renewal and regeneration,
keep us holy-hearted.
May we make sacred the meal,
the breaking of bread,
the laughter of friendship.
May we make sacred each moment,
connecting us to what is most important,
most vital, most essential.

Break new ground in us.
Push us up through hardened surfaces
and let us grow green, be raised again,
that what has deadened in us
will return to a newness of life
and flower again.

Amen

Prayer to the Mystery of the Resurrection

O Beloved Spirit,
From the beginning of what we claim to know of the human,
we unearth elaborate rituals commemorating death
and we discover ancient, sacred essences ensuring continuity.
And now, 6000, 50,000, 200,000 years of the human,
yet we are none the wiser, but like our ancestors
can only second guess what awaits behind death's door.
This knowledge of our impending death
combined with this not-knowing beyond our death,
mixes with this prayer of breath we call life
intoxicating us with the mystery of both our before and our after
combined with the magnificence and grace of our now.

How far back do our genetic roots reach
in order to reel in this eye color, body type and stature?
How deep do our minds extend when reeling in
such fearful archetypes, such heroic dreams,
such breakthroughs and insights?
How true is the true of us
as we reel in the in-formed original of us
unencumbered by opinions and goals?

Do You keep us in the dark so that we might know light?
Do You separate us from us that we might know union?
Do You taint us with anger and despair
that we might know the pure of love and beloving?
All that we can infer is embedded in the cycle of this life
and we bear witness that there is power in the resurrection—
that in the death of the seed, the bloom of the fruit.
Like our ancestors we carry in our essences of faith, hope and love,
unmistakable like the scent of frankincense, cinnamon and cloves
and all we know for sure, is the greatest of these is love
as it sustains and nourishes our soul with body;
and, we pray, will sustain and nourish our soul without body.
Amen

Prayer to the Boundless Within Our Borders

O Beloved Spirit,
Bounded in a border of skin, we bump against the mystery of life
revealed through our touching upon friendship, laughter, and delight;
revealed through our hearing of music, song, and poetry;
revealed through our seeing art, dance, and craftsmanship.
How large grows the rim of what we do not know
as our growing knowledge expands
the borders of what remains for us to discover.
The mystery engulfs us with its boundlessness
and we marvel at being alive, awake, of breathing in and taking in.
We enter into a ceaseless river of amazement
and offer You our joy in response to
the boundless within our borders—
this most generous, most beneficent gift we call life.

Bounded in a border of time, we bump against the mystery of death.
Revealed through the shortness of our breath here,
of our time with parents and family, with those we hold dear.
Revealed through the quickness of our days here,
the pace of seasonal change, the blooms on the ground.
Revealed through the "one" chance we have to explore and to be.
How large grows the rim of what we do not know
as our growing knowledge expands
the borders of what we cannot know.
The mystery engulfs us with its boundlessness
and we marvel at being so close to death, so free of body,
of breathing out and letting go.
We enter into a ceaseless river of amazement
and offer You our joy in response to
the boundless within our borders—
this most generous, most beneficent gift we call death.

Bounded by borders of skin and of time,
we look to take this time, this skin in this life;
to explore the holy, the amazing, the miraculous
that these may be the very essences that fill all our days.
Amen

Creativity

What if God awaits from man
a feat of free creativeness
and demands of man the manifestation of all
the powers with which he is endowed?
This is the will of God, and man must fulfill it.

Nikolai Berdyaev

Prayer for a Day Like No Other

O Beloved Spirit,
Not just another day, but a day like no other.
Not another awakening but an awakening full of surprise.
Not another appointment but a divine appointment here by grace.
This day—how ripe with the fruit of so many days before.
This day—how pregnant with so many awakenings until now.
This day—how potent with so many appointments
infilling this current hour.

Earth-time, sacred-time, *chronos* and *kairos* time:
our palette of a day taking a spin around a fiery star.
Our one chance to be:
to become, to behold, to be fully awake, to see.
Awaken in us a spirit of creation, our *Imago Dei*,
that we might answer the call of the Human:
to make sacred, to make play, to make new,
to make whole, to make beautiful—to Create!

No other day than *this* day.
No other awakening than *this* awakening.
No other appointment than *this* appointment.
We have been brought to this moment like no other moment—
by prophetic dreams, by inspired faith, by cadence and color.

Here we are in the current of time, awash in the now,
alive in the new.
And hidden in this day, the *Imago Dei*
scattered across our earthen cells.
Unearth this *Imago Dei* impressioned on our hearts,
that our acts of creation will make known the potent potential
embedded in the *Imago* of this one more day—
this one more day in which
to make sacred, to make play, to make new,
to make whole, to make beautiful—to Create!
Amen

Prayer for the Original

O Beloved Spirit,
Hear us in our comfort
and our need to be comfortable.
Hear us in our holding on
and our need to hold on.
Hear us in our successes
and our need to be successful.
We are endangered.
Hear us.

Hear us in all our doings
and our need to be doing.
Hear us in all our things
and our need to have things.
Hear us in all our busyness
and our need to be busy.
We are endangered.
Hear us.

We are in danger that the Original
will be tainted by what we think we should be.
We are in danger that the Creative
will be stymied by what we think we should do.
We are in danger that the True
will be undone by what we think will please another.

We are endangered.
Hear us.
Clear the way to our Original.
Raise us anew.

Amen

Prayer for the Excellent Mind

O Beloved Spirit,
Let me not fear
that what I cultivate in my mind
will un-source what grows in my heart.
Let me not fear that what I think
will undermine what I strive to unite.
Let me not fear that what I discover
will fragment what I strive to envision.

For so long, I have been suspicious of the excellent mind;
that it would disqualify me from oneness,
that it would hurl me long and far
from your garden of conversation.

Re-source me now that I may take the fuel
of great ideas and great achievements
and shape my intellect with their passion.
Re-source me now that I may break
the barrier of my halting discomfort
and tap the power of the generative mind.
Re-source me now
that what waters my psyche and fuels my thoughts
will not be hampered by my pride
nor constricted by my fear of pride.

Instead, ever source me to the generative
that what flows through my intellect
flows full of fire,
flows full of vision,
flows full of *Logos*.

Amen

Prayer for What We Have Not Seen Before

O Beloved Spirit,
There are no fixes,
no corrections to be made—
only waves of pain and joy upon which to ride.

There are no bandages big enough,
no sutures strong enough—
just a wealth of colors with which to mix and play.

There are no straight lines to sustain,
just the briefest of openings—
only moments in which to listen, to sing, to let go with love.

We are too often duped into a "right" way,
tortured by the hint of a wrong choice.
Instead, let us attack the canvas
with a breakout of color
and bring our joy to this creative adventure
as we discover a new revelation of the unseen.

Amen

Prayer for Exuberance

O Beloved Spirit,
Teach me the craft of exuberance.
Teach me the Book of Kells
where coiling colors
unleash flowering circles
within flowering circles,
and ceaselessly flow into the filigree
of the first letter
of the first word
of the first sentence,
blooming into the phrase,
"In the beginning was the *Logos*."

Teach me the Book of Kells
with a design that dizzies the eye,
with a truth that puzzles the mind.
Emblazoned with a sacred reason;
it is not what it says, but what it is
and continues to do.
The truth etched into the flowing lines
of an exuberant labyrinth
spilling eternally out
into the eternal Beginning of the *Logos*.

In my ways of worship,
in my words of meditation,
teach me the art of exuberance—
teach me the Book of Kells.

Amen

Prayer to Music Unfathomed

O Beloved Spirit,
You are the breath
that elates our hearts with joy
and pleasures our voices
with a song of amazing mystery.
We resound with Your music unfathomed.

What marvelous, elusive ways You have with us
as we delight in the beauty of unknowing.
We think You are at play with us
and at play within us
and at play through us.

You are the breath
that elates our hearts with joy
and pleasures our voices
with a song of amazing mystery.
We resound with Your music unfathomed.

Play us, O Beloved Spirit,
and let our stops give way to Your soundings
and let us go in love,
and let us go in love,
and let us go in love,
as You play through us
and as You play us
and as You play.

Amen

Prayer for the Vital

O Beloved Spirit,
awake in us whatsoever is vital, alive, creative—
vital silence that stirs active the imagination,
vital action that fires into a *caritas*, a spirit of love,
vital creation that surprises with its rhythm, its color, its humor.
Awake in us whatsoever is vital, alive, creative.
Too long a season of dread.
Too long a drought of spirit.
Too long a fear of a misstep.
Awake in us whatsoever is vital, alive, creative.

O Beloved Spirit, rid us of the self-conscious
that we may fulfill Your spirit with a spirit-filling.
Rid us of the God that anchors us to our past
that we may inspire the God beyond the God
and in this inspiration—a deification of You in us.
Too long a season of arid belief unhinged from our beloving.
Too long a time of forgoing our chance to be.
Too long a choiceless choice to react and not to see.
Awake in us whatsoever is vital, alive, creative.

May we rise to our place to shine.
May we rise to the call of a new song.
May we sing the joy to be alive, to be awake.

O Beloved Spirit, awake in us
whatsoever is vital, alive, creative—
vital silence that stirs active the imagination,
vital action that fires into a *caritas*—a spirit of love,
vital creation that surprises with its rhythm, its color, its humor.
Awake in us whatsoever is vital, alive, creative.
Amen

Prayer to Singing Up the Sun

O Beloved Spirit,
Let us sing up the sun and live as suns—
as radiant, glory-filled beings
where Your Divine intersects our animal
and grows in heart,
    in soul,
        in intelligence,
            in feeling and in will.
Let us bring renown to You
who is made known through us.

Amen

Prayer to a Most Magnificent Creation

O Beloved Spirit,
With the raw ingredients of this day,
let us knead the mixture of what is at work in us
and generate a most magnificent creation—
awakening our essence and calling it into being,
arousing our love and invoking its presence,
stimulating our imagination and let it just play.
We are more than what we do,
more than the role we fill, more than the title we wear.
We are the dance, the one chance; the only chance
for You to see through us, for You to hear through us,
for You to know through us, for You to love through us.

With the raw ingredients of this day,
let us inspire a creation full of inventiveness
and generate a most magnificent creation—
transforming the mundane into the surprising,
the mortifications into new possibilities,
the falling short into the leaping ahead.
We are more than what we do,
more than the role we fill, more than the title we wear.
We are the dance, the one chance; the only chance
for You to see through us, for You to hear through us,
for You to know through us, for You to love through us.

With the raw ingredients of this day,
let us expound into an expression of unmistakable soul
and generate a most magnificent creation—
finding what is core to us and giving it color,
finding what is innate to us and giving it music,
finding what is impressioned on our hearts and giving it life.
We are more than what we do,
more than the role we fill, more than the title we wear,
we are the dance, the one chance; the only chance
for You to see through us, for You to hear through us,
for You to know through us, for You to love through us.
Amen

Prayer in Praise of the Unlikely

O Beloved Spirit,
From the unexpected voice, from the most unlikely of places,
from the charismatic fire descending like a dove,
affirmations of Your love, of the sacred in this time,
of a mission, to create.

O Beloved Spirit, may we embrace the genius
seeded in us from the beginning.
May we breathe the breath You inspire
into our dreams and into our imagination.
May we catch fire with Your fire—unafraid of fierce
or our own Only Begotten. Let us create!

O Beloved Spirit, on a hill, on a bench, in an upper room,
with a pen, with a brush, with a stringed instrument,
on a blank page, on an open canvas, on a score of staffs
waiting for signature and notation,
of a mission, to create.

O Beloved Spirit, from the unexpected voice,
from the most unlikely of places,
from the charismatic fire descending like a dove,
affirmations of Your love, of the sacred in this time,
of a mission, to create.

O Beloved Spirit, let us sing the new song that sings up the sun,
that intones the beloving,
that sings of the hearing in the sight
and of the insight in the hearing
of a mission, to create.

O Beloved Spirit, let us see and be seen.
Let us hear and be heard.
Let us hear and choose the fiery song of You—
our enraptured new song of Holy Spirit. Let us create!
Amen

Prayer for the Unmistakable

O Beloved Spirit,
In response to Your creation,
a creative response from us.
That from the place where we are,
we are unmistakable,
that is, like no one else—
in the way that:
we lead,
we decide,
we build,
we dream.

Amen

Prayer for Ecclesia

O Beloved Spirit,
It is but a baby—
fragile yet vital, young yet ancient,
not place but person,
very much who, little of what.

It is but a baby—
fleshed out through the thoughts we bring,
the prayers we write, the candles we light,
the music we make.

It is but a baby—
in its birth, our birth;
in its need, our need;
in its fruit, our sustenance for Spirit.

It awakens us in our night
and with its cries it calls us to our joy.
It is not easy; yet, it is worthy.

Through it we learn worship—
not a recitation of praise
rather a way to create as community,
a way to aspire as one,
a way to vision the highest in the Human,
both before us and within us.
It is us and yet, greater than us.

It is of the breath that spoke,
"Let there be light."
Its power is the creative.
Its call, to create.
This ecclesia, itself, our creation
and we in turn, its creation.

O Beloved Spirit, grant us a great measure of wisdom
as we nurture what has been born.
We marvel at what has been given us
and pray that it may grow as it is to grow.

Amen

Joy

Love is an Infinite Sea whose skies are a bubble of foam,
know that it is the waves of Love that turn the wheels of Heaven:
without Love, nothing in the world would have life.
How is an inorganic thing transformed into a plant?
How are plants sacrificed to become rich with spirit?
How is spirit sacrificed to become Breath,
one scent of which is potent enough to make Mary pregnant?
Every single atom is drunk on this Perfection and runs towards It,
and what does this running secretly say but "Glory be to God!"

Rumi

Prayer of Joy

O Beloved Spirit,
I am wedged between walls
that will not budge.

I am at the base of mountains
that will not move.

I am stuck beneath clouds
seamed with threatening rain.

And yet, despite those conditions,
I know a joy—
a joy without conditions,
a joy that sustains me
even when my passage is blocked
and my days seem sterile.

This unconditional joy rides
upon the intake of my breath
and circulates a rejuvenating life.

You are that breath,
my joy—
that life.

Amen

Prayer for Here

O Beloved Spirit,
I seek to surrender to You my longing for You
that I might take root in what is here
and not in what I wish.
I seek to surrender my seeking for You
to avoid reflecting what it is I want to find
instead of finding what is here.
Where is here?
And why is here so hard to find?

My longing speaks of a separation
from that which is unknowable.
My joy speaks of a union
with that which is unspeakable.
My longing seems to say, "I must come closer."
My joy seems to say, "You are in me and I in You."
Do I surrender my longing so my joy may be made full
or is my longing but the warp to the woof of my joy,
and in their weave, Your humorous, Human design?
I desire You and yet, You are here.
To find the You in the Here,
it would seem I must give up
my desire for You here and now
and in all hereafters.

And so my pain in my longing is
but right angle to the laughter in my joy.
And in my longing and in my joy,
my love for Your bright design.
I long for Here even though the joy of Here is all I have.
Amen

Prayer for Joy in Tough Times

O Beloved Spirit,
When we find ourselves in an intersection where we are confronted
with the unexpected, the disappointing, the unfair;
when we find ourselves in an intersection where we are stymied
with too much to consider and not enough means to clarify;
when we find ourselves in an intersection where we can't decide,
can't move forward, can't determine which way to head;
when we find ourselves in this muddle of an intersection,
in this bewilder-ness, re-member us with joy,
re-sound within us with joy, re-juvenate us with joy.

When we find ourselves in an intersection
where what we had hoped for is intercepted
with the unanticipated, the puzzling, the confusing;
when we find ourselves in the midst of the unsettling,
confronted with choices to be made yet no assurance of a right choice;
when we find ourselves in the midst of a snarl
with no easy way forward,
when we find ourselves in this muddle of an intersection,
in this bewilder-ness, re-member us with joy,
re-sound within us with joy, re-juvenate us with joy.

Re-turn us to the simple, the joy of breath and breathing.
Re-turn us to the simple, the joy of song and singing.
Re-turn us to the simple, the joy of creation and creating.
The universe dances across our skies in a coming together of stars
laden with light from so many millennia ago.
The earth dances under our feet in a coming together of where we
have been and where we are going—in a most sacred choreography.
Let us take what is most difficult in this crossroads of ours
and submit to the simple,
to the dance,
to the joyous,
to the marvelous,
to the mystery of being alive.

Amen

Prayer to Transform the Unexpected

O Beloved Spirit,
We are reminded that we are vulnerable to the unexpected—
to the painful, to the unpleasant, to the unfair.
We are reminded that we are vulnerable to the unexpected—
to the ebbs, to the downturns, to the gnarly.
We are reminded that we are vulnerable to the unexpected—
to the hurtful, to the costly, to times forsaken.
No amount of prayer, or blissful affirmations, or positive thinking
insulates us from the fact and the impact of the unexpected.

And we look to you, O Beloved Spirit, for an exhalation,
for the release of Your breath to re-enliven our unexpected
through a detoxifying expiration of the bitter,
through a welcome outflowing of the disappointing,
through a letting go of all that has bound us
to what we thought the unexpected should and would be.
So we look to you, O Beloved Spirit, for inspiration, for Your breath
to stimulate our experience with a fresh intake of newness
a fresh infilling of nourishment and replenishment,
a fresh inhalation of vitality and healing.

We pray now as we consider the unexpected in our life
and in the lives of those we love—
that Your breath will infill us with the fullness of joy even
by way of the tough inflections of sorrow, disappointment and loss.
We pray now as we consider the unexpected in our life
and in the lives of those we love—
that the unexpected will be transformed into nourishment for the soul
and replenish us with the surprise of more joy.

We are reminded at this time to look to you, O Beloved Spirit,
for inspiration, for expiration—for the mix of Your breath
with our unexpected so that we might know the joy of joy.
We are ever grateful for Your transforming breath,
for the exhilarating experience of joy,
for the possibility of joy by way of the unexpected.

Amen

Prayer to Becoming an Instrument of Joy

O Beloved Spirit,
Not just an instrument of knowledge,
not just a creature of senses,
not just a body of experience;
instead we are a soul-filled *enthusiasmos*.
We are an amazing breath of fresh spirit inspired.
We are vitalized by Your breath
circulated through our instrument of knowledge,
through our creaturely senses,
through our body of experience.
Through Your breath inspired in us,
we know soul, we are soul,
and it is soul we aspire and inspire to know and become.

O Beloved Spirit, what a joy to know this joy.
What a joy to en-joy and to nurture this joy in us.
Soul fill us,
though much of our day is lost to the mundane.
Soul fill us,
though much of our time is spent on what seems small.
Soul fill us,
though we are lost in what must be done next.

O Beloved Spirit, we are grateful not to be
just an instrument of knowledge,
just a creature of senses,
just a body of experience.
Accept our joy for this infilling of joy.

Amen

Prayer for Emptiness

O Beloved Spirit,
As more and more luxuries
convert into daily necessities,
we realize no amount of comfort
can insulate us from our need for joy.

No matter how sophisticated our setting,
no matter how established our knowledge,
no matter how full our days,
we realize no amount of attainment
can replace our need for emptiness.

Teach us empty,
that we might have a place for joy to fill.
Teach us empty,
that we might release what holds us.
Teach us empty,
that we might experience for the first time again,
and then again.

In the midst of all our achievements
and all our things and all the things we do well,
bless us with being empty.
For out of our emptiness comes empathy—
and out of our empathy, love—
and out of our love, joy.

Fill us with Your emptiness.

Amen

Prayer of Rapture

O Beloved Spirit,
Enraptured with the marvel of being alive
and with the infilling of Your fiery love—
we are alight with joy.

Enraptured with the harvest of friendship,
marriage, intimacy, worship, community, family—
we are charged with joy.

Enraptured with the wonder of discovering,
creating, singing, playing, writing, reading—
we embark with joy.

This great communion of inspiration,
this taking in of the vital breath of Your spirit—
this tasting, seeing, hearing, smelling, touching
of what has been inspired into and through the earth of us—
lights us up with joy.

O Beloved Spirit, so brief this dance,
this inspired breath, this time to touch—
so brief a moment— so brief the bloom.
For the bounty of this earth
and all its wonderment,
we are grateful.
For our mothers and fathers and our teachers
and all that they have given,
we are grateful.

Let us, this day,
be alight with joy, be charged with joy, embark with joy.
Amen

Prayer to the Spirit That Rivers Through Us

O Beloved Spirit,
As You river through our lives
and move us with Your current of wonder,
we are upended with the immensity of this inspired life.
As You river through our lives
and move us with Your current of joy,
we are flooded with a gratefulness we cannot contain—
a gratefulness that spills out of us in music and dance and poetry
and song and prayer and friendship.
As You river through our lives
and move us with Your current of empathic love,
we are awash with the richness of the moment—
a moment flooded by a touch, a knowing,
a wave of laughter, tears—a glimpse of soul.

O Beloved Spirit, as You river through our lives
and move us with the current of Your wonder,
the current of Your joy, the current of Your love,
we are ecstatically carried by the mystery of knowing You
through this body we have been given,
by the mystery of knowing You
through the gifts in which You have entrusted us,
by the mystery of knowing You
by way of this planet where You have placed us.

O Beloved Spirit, no ocean of words, no sounding of song,
no onrush of praise can express
one ten-thousandth part of the bounties
which You have bestowed upon us.
No choreography of expression,
no unceasing dialogue of adoration,
no wealth of color and form can express
one ten-thousandth part of the current
with which You river through our lives.
We are enraptured by the marvel of Your inspiration
and carry that rapture into the very breath of the breath we breathe.
Amen

Prayer of Joy to the World

O Beloved Spirit,
Sing us, dance us, play us—
transform our joy into song, into movement, into rhythm—
into a lilt in our voice, into a gait in our step,
into a cadence in our sound.
We swim in a sea of madness spawned, procreated, generated
through a groaning, a beloving, an omnificent sounding
channeled through millions of millions of years.
Now seen, now awakened, in this moment through stars,
through layers of eons embedded in the labyrinth of caves,
through an omnipresent love seamed in a baby's smile,
in a child wrapped in our arms, in an evening with a friend.

Sing us, dance us, play us—
transform our joy into song, into movement, into rhythm.
We glory in the glorious, in the paradoxical, in the riveting
madness of atoms dancing through forests and flowers,
through cascades and waterfalls, through summits and canyons,
spawned, procreated, generated
through a groaning, a beloving, an omnificent sounding
channeled through millions of millions of years.
Now seen, now awakened, in this moment, this Holy Here
where we have been charged, lit up, enlivened with our one chance
to live, to shine, to know again for the first time
the reverence of, the awe of, the mystery of
the breath within the breath, the heart within the heart,
the Holy of Holies in our own magnificent temple—
our one chance to become and to be Human.

O amazing madness that dances through our bodies,
sing us, dance us, play us—
transform our joy into song, into movement, into rhythm.
We are a channel for Your groaning, Your beloving,
Your omnificent sounding—
now seen, now awakened, in this moment.
now seen, now awakened, in this magnificent temple.
now seen, now awakened, in this Holy Here.
Amen

Prayer of Entheos

O Beloved Spirit,
I dedicate this day to the *entheos*.
Open wide the conduit of light
and let the morning become awake in me.

Let this day's dispensation of Spirit
have its way with me.

Winged Fire, Holy Breath, combust within me and take flight.
Infused into the events of this day—*entheos*—
God at work in me and
God at work through me.

Amen

Prayer in Response to Joy

O Beloved Spirit,
On the inside of the Inside, in the kernel of the Kernel,
in the center of the Center,
a joy-struck pitch, a tuning vibration,
an initiating utterance resonating in play,
in mirth, in bathing oscillations of beloving.

Let the song thrilling through us recite this joyous opus.
Let us learn to be played and in turn, learn to play attuned to joy.
A holy hilarity seems to spill out into a profusion of colors and scents
and tastes—into an onrush of sounds and touches.
Let us, in a rich vibrato, echo in antiphonal response as we unfold
in song, in dance, *in music heard so deeply that it is not heard at all—*
for we are the music for as long as the music lasts.

We are astounded by the impossibility
that seams this moment with all moments
and inhabits our finiteness with its infinity.
Our quest: to hold and to hallow the immensity
of at-one-ness, of at-once-ness,
in the center of the heart of our heart—
to be fully awake to the beloving;
to sustain the pulsating ecstasy of being;
to withstand the potent paradox of being human.

On the inside of the Inside, in the kernel of the Kernel,
in the center of the Center, a joy-struck pitch, a tuning vibration,
an initiating utterance resounding in play,
in mirth, in bathing oscillations of beloving.

Let us sing a rousing new song
that explicates and expounds and expands
upon that vibratory pitch that set us into motion—
that unfathomable Word, that ineffable *Logos*,
that all-encompassing *aum* finding its way through us.
Amen

Prayer to the Madness of Joy

O Beloved Spirit,
There is madness in this moment—
a riot of color and sound,
a rebellion of wind and clouds,
a startling outbreak of growth topped with glorious blooms,
a tempestuous season wrestling to spring free
from the grip and gripes of winter.

There is madness in this moment—
a riot of conflicted expectations,
a rebellion of whimsy and willfulness,
a startling breakthrough of inborn discoveries,
a tempestuous time of too much and yet, not enough wherewithal—
a time seeded with change and with more change.

There is madness in this moment—
a laughter unearthing our attachments
releasing them into intoxicating light,
a breathtaking beauty replenishing our depleted vision,
a brazen newness sprouting in
our most stubborn and unyielding of places.

There is madness in this moment—
dancing in daylight,
blazing in flings of flames,
enthusing and infusing our veins.
We are unearthed by the dance of joy
seaming all the disconnectedness.
We are rejuvenated by the dance of joy
reverberating through our hearts, drawing us into closer union.
We are unleashed by the dance of joy
enlivening our imaginations and jolting us into an awake-ness.

For the madness of the moment—
for the joy in each morsel,
for the rejuvenation of the season, we are grateful.
Amen

I Am

The seed of God is in us.
If the seed had a good, wise and industrious cultivator,
it would thrive all the more and grow up to God whose seed it is
and the fruit would be equal to the nature of God.
Now the seed of a pear tree grows into a pear tree,
a hazel seed into a hazel tree,
the seed of God into God.

Meister Eckhart

Prayer from the Burning Bush

O Beloved Spirit,
What a marvelous sight fills our eyes,
what a surprising love is placed in our hearts,
what an amazing creation is woven into our very being.
Great gusts of Spirit abound and inspiration
infiltrates the imagination.
You call us by name and look to us by name
and we hope to escalate by name the I am
that inhabits our I Am at its core.

What an astonishing place we have been given to live.
What an astounding hope fills our hearts and our minds.
What a joyous dance plays out through the earth of us.
Your onrush of fiery tongues fills us with the impossible.
You call us by name and look to us by name.
And You call out the name that inhabits our I Am at its core.

What a grace-filled ocean surrounds us.
What a wide, ever-changing canvas envelops us.
What a most arresting beauty upends us.
And in Your voice, the imperative: “Be my voice.”
And in Your fire, the imperative: “Be my vision.”
And in Your birth, the imperative: “Be my beloved.”
You call us by name and look to us by name.
And You call out the name that inhabits our I Am at its core.
Amen

Prayer to Grow Soul

O Beloved Spirit,
Implanted deep in this cellular temple, the seed of God—
spark divine, insight, imagination.
Implanted deep in this cellular temple, the seed of God—
the impetus to explore, to create, to be more than we are.
Implanted deep in this cellular temple, the seed of God—
the vision to dream, to invent, to make new again.
Enthuse us with the necessary joy to nurture, to love,
to belove this soul we have been given to grow.

Implanted deep in this cellular temple, the sprout of God—
cooking, planting, writing, painting.
Implanted deep in this cellular temple, the sprout of God—
racing, singing, reading, sculpting.
Implanted deep in this cellular temple, the sprout of God—
dancing, solving, researching, healing.
Enthuse us with the necessary joy to nurture, to love,
to belove this soul we have been given to grow.

Implanted deep in this cellular temple, the bloom of God—
friendship, compassion, forgiveness.
Implanted deep in this cellular temple, the bloom of God—
fire of mind, an enlightened heart, the ecstasy of union.
Implanted deep in this cellular temple, the bloom of God—
unceasing dialogue with all that is sacred and universal.
Enthuse us with the necessary joy to nurture, to love,
to belove this soul we have been given to grow.

Let us rejoice in the pear seed that becomes the pear tree.
Let us rejoice in the acorn that becomes an oak tree.
And let us rejoice in the God seed implanted deep in this cellular temple
that becomes the God tree.
Enthuse us with the necessary joy to nurture, to love,
to belove this soul we have been given to grow.

Amen

Prayer for New Vision

O Beloved Spirit,
Do not despair of me,
though it seems
I am so long in breaking through.

Do not despair of me,
though this snarl of flesh
seems to constrict my own I Am.

Do not despair of me,
though I seem to shape what I see
with what I expect—
always seeing two where there is only one.

Do not despair of me
though I seem to take pride in my trying—
stubbed off from my becoming.

I cannot roll away the stone
or widen the aperture for Your light.
I look to You for grace,
for an opening into new vision,
new eyes.

Do not despair of me.
Your grace, my only hope.

Amen

Prayer to the Unbound Boundary

O Beloved Spirit,
The ground is charged with ancient voices
trapped in monoliths of stone, and bones upon bones
lie buried in barrows under our feet.
And the boundary of the very mystery of the mystery we celebrate
grows ever deeper, ever wider, ever higher than we ever imagined.

What Creative power has invoked us into life,
firing up our first cries as its Holy Breath combusts within us?
What Holy Other, what Mother of Earth
has called us to this life of love and struggle
that we might know life and love and struggle?
The sky is charged with unknown voices
tucked into the cloak of a sunlit radiance.
What life lies outside the life we know as life
and interrupts our sleep with other hierarchies, other-worldly dreams?

What Creative power calls us to our death
and brings us to our one last burn of an exhale?
What Holy Other, what Mother of Earth
receives our flesh and bones from this life of love and struggle
and sets us on a journey beyond this journey?
By name You call us out from the comfort of what we have always
known and charge us with the fiery call to Create!

This unbound boundary of what we do not and cannot know,
embeds us in an ever dizzying display of the marvelous,
an ever dazzling drama of the dark and of the light,
an ever upending dynamic of the earth and of the stars.
And the boundary of the very mystery of the mystery we celebrate
grows ever deeper, ever wider, ever higher than we ever imagined.

O Beloved Spirit, we have no recourse
but to delight in the delight that is Here,
and to embrace the embrace of the love we have come here to know,
and to create the stars that are uniquely ours, waiting to be.
Amen

Prayer for Inner Harmony

O Beloved Spirit,
From the outside,
there are so many threads—
so many threads to combine and unify,
so many threads to take care of and follow.
From the outside, so many threads entangle,
snarl and ensnare.

From the inside, there is but one pattern to unfold,
but one voice to invoke,
but one rhythm to synchronize.
From the inside, there is only the one,
a singular source that restores and fulfills.

Far too often, I stray from this singular vision,
disconnect from the center of my one.
Far too often, I feel only the frenzy of too many threads
with not enough time to do them right.
In my contemplative moments,
I know that it is only in the only that I am whole
and when I am swirling in the many,
I am tangled and undone.

In times of clarity, I realize that I do not have the time
to fuss with the time I do not have.
Let the threaded efforts of my trying
align with the pattern of my I am
that all that I am weaves from the inside
all the threads I thought were mine to sort.

Amen

Prayer at Christening

O Beloved Spirit,
Into this present moment, full of Newness,
arrives this presence, full of Newness,
still fragrant from her Before,
still fresh in her joy and discovery.

And thus we observe:
seed to root to plant to flower to seed—
earth to bloom to earth to seed—
a soul is born into our midst
carrying in an essence unmistakable,
like the scent of cinnamon or clove or lilac.
How grateful we are to re-experience
the experience of new life
through this newly-named, new life.

Into this present, full of Nowness—
given name, and family name—
comes this presence, full of Newness,
bearing an eternal name
carrying in a lineage of Spirit.
We welcome and embrace this newly-named, new life
and honor the names she has taken on
as well as the name that she has brought in with her.

All names, known and unknown,
we embrace with our joy,
that her rich inheritance will be
a life enriched with a life-long beloving.
How grateful we are to re-experience
the experience of new life
through this newly-named, new life.
In great gratitude.

Amen

Prayer to the Alchemy of the Human

O Beloved Spirit,
How vital Your breath to my breath, my Beloved.
How vital Your breath to my heart, my Beloved.
How vital Your breath to my song, my Beloved.
How vital Your I am to my Becoming.
How vital Your joy to my dance—
this one chance to dance like no other.

In the secret chamber of our coming together,
infiltrate the atrium of my heart
and sustain it with Your fire.
In the secret chamber of our coming together,
infiltrate the altar of my will
and unite my breath with Your breath.
In the secret chamber of our coming together,
infiltrate the dark roots of my dreams and my desires
and articulate through them the rejuvenating waters of our embrace.
How vital my I am to the Becoming.
How vital my joy to the dance,
this one chance to dance like no other.

In the secret chamber of our coming together,
stir me up with all that must be done,
mix me up with all that already Is.
Fill my action with Your sacred vision,
in this one chance to dance like no other.
Sustain the alchemy of my daily work with Your holy fire,
in this one chance to dance like no other.

How vital my breath to Your breath, my Beloved.
How vital my breath to Your heart, my Beloved.
How vital my breath to Your song, my Beloved.
How vital my I am to the Becoming.
How vital my joy to the dance,
this one chance to dance like no other.

Amen

Prayer for the Source

O Beloved Spirit,
Not from the peripheral
but from my source—
the words I speak.

Not from the peripheral
but from my source—
the actions I accomplish.

Not from the peripheral
but from my source—
the vision I hone.

Not from the shallow,
but from deep breath.
Not from the momentary,
but from timeless thinking.
Not from the wind-tossed,
but from the ground of me.

Though my pace be on the run,
may my heart be rooted to the source.

How can I bear light
if it is not the light innate to my seed—
deep-soiled and soul-rich?
May the lineage
of Your light in my seed
take root not in the peripheral
but in my source.

Amen

Prayer for the Potential

O Beloved Spirit,
We are an outer circumference
inscribing an infinite center—
our potential.
At times, this center radiates outward
and through our actions.
At times, this center collapses inward
and leaves us separate.
Our sin—not in what we have done wrong
but in what we cannot seem to tap.
Our hell—not in the torment of our errors
but in the separation we feel from our center.
We do not seek an eternal life
that begins on the day we die,
rather we seek an immersion
into the eternal of our now and here,
our potential, here and now.

Reconcile our outer to our eternal,
our action to our possibility.
Let today's sin and tomorrow's hell
die in our death now,
that we may be united with life eternal,
with the infinitude of our potential.

Amen

Prayer for the Unbounded

O Beloved Spirit,
Only so many breaths,
only so many heartbeats,
animate this life to which
I ascribe my name.
In the shortness of my breaths,
the longing for a link between
my life, now bound by time,
and my life unbounded.

Only so many breaths,
only so many heartbeats,
measure out a rhythm
for this singular song I sing.
In the quickness of the beats
the longing for a link
between what life is lost to me
and the life I gain in the losing.

You have sealed from my sight
my before and my after and yet,
a light shines through all my days.
In the shortness of my breaths,
and in the quickness of my heartbeats,
my longing for a link
between the light in my days now
and Your light always.
May it be so.

Amen

Prayer for the Imago Deo

O Beloved Spirit,
We are born with an unborn image
layered beneath our flesh—
the potential to be Human.
We search our days
for the means and grace
to penetrate and release the greater.

Lead us to those men and women
who through the ages found their passion
and blended it with the *Imago Deo.*
Lead us to those men and women
whose very model can inspire us
to reveal our own, deeper image of Human.

Amen

Prayer for the Lighting of a Candle

O Beloved Spirit,
A candle is lit to nourish the soul's journey
and we are left with a big sigh of breath
as the essence we knew by name moves out and on.
Surely there is joy in the leaving behind, in the letting go.
We pray that we may keep centered in this prayer—
this conversation with the imaginative, the amazing, the beautiful.
O these Holy days—of time with friends, teachers and family!
How grateful we are for our all-too-brief
excursion in body, in time and in place.

A candle is lit to nourish the soul's journey
and we are left with a big sigh of breath
as the essence we knew by name moves out and on.
Surely there is joy packed into the bundle of days we call our life.
We pray that we may keep centered in this prayer—
this conversation with the color-filled, the timeless, the true.
O these Holy days—of striving, of praying, of singing!
How grateful we are for our all-too-brief
dance of tasting, touching, smelling, seeing, hearing.

A candle is lit to nourish the soul's journey
and we are left with a big sigh of breath
as the essence we knew by name moves out and on.
Surely there is joy in the reunion with those waiting beyond us.
We pray that we may keep centered in this prayer—
this conversation with an essence
we knew and hope to know still more.
O these Holy days—of walking uprightly,
of insights, of imaginings!
How grateful we are for our all-too-brief
days of work and play, of dreams and disappointments.

Let us light a candle this day to nourish the soul's journey,
to fortify our days here on Earth with a love that does not die,
to secure our essence in this one chance to be and to become.
Amen

Yang

When Moses threw the wand into the Red Sea,
the sea, quite contrary to the expected miracle,
did not divide itself to leave a dry passage for the Jews.
Not until the first man had jumped into the sea
did the promised miracle happen and the waves recede.

Jewish legend

Prayer of Yang

O Beloved Spirit,
Heaven above, heaven below. Ch'ien over Ch'ien.
Three unbroken lines over three unbroken lines.
The Chinese hexagram for Yang, the creative.
Its attribute, action; its image, heaven.
Yang, the creative—the perfect complement to Yin, the receptive.
Its power, the generative; its glory, perseverance in what is right.
The receptive gives birth; the creative initiates.

Three unbroken lines above. Ch'ien above.
Three unbroken lines below. Ch'ien below.
Heaven above—a begetting of all things.
Heaven below—an arousing force to reawaken.
Joined together, the six unbroken lines form Jacob's ladder.
Joined together, six strong rungs that lead upwards to the creative.
And so we invoke the power of the Yang
where we wrestle our angel and square off till daybreak,
where we hold fast to what we believe to be right,
where we persevere and will not let go until we receive the blessing.

And so we invoke the power of the Yang—
the generative power of beginnings, the *potentia* in the moment.
And from its seed, a way of striving, a way of persevering.
And through this fierce wrestling of our angels—
new wine, new words, new birth, new spirit.
Three unbroken lines above. Ch'ien above.
Three unbroken lines below. Ch'ien below.
Heaven above—a begetting of all things.
Heaven below—an arousing force that reawakens.

O Beloved Spirit, pair our need to be still, to listen, to receive
with our longing to be more, to create, to achieve.
Teach us the three unbroken lines above,
placed over the three unbroken lines below
that we may attain to the heaven in us,
and achieve the best in us.

Amen

Prayer of Seeking

O Beloved Spirit,
Our search for You is certain death
unless we seek to die.
Answers stand in stagnant pools
while unknowing fuels a living fire.

Burn up the words we worship
yet infuse us with their passion.
Unfasten us from our finding
that we might be naked in our seeking.

Kindle our death,
that life may quicken in its wake.

Amen

Prayer to Be All In

O Beloved Spirit,
O Breath of Fire,
We are charged with fire to lie down in Fire.
Not removed but all in,
not sprinkled but immersed.

On earth to unearth:
    hidden treasures, wells of fire, veins of gold.
On earth to birth:
    dance, music, new song.
On earth to reveal:
    beauty, delight, grandeur.

O Breath of Fire,
We are charged with fire to lie down in Fire.
Not removed but all in,
not sprinkled but immersed,

Not dismissing but embracing:
    the sightings, the visions, the breakthroughs.
Not dismissing but embracing:
    the deaths, the disappointments, the unwanted, the uninvited.
Not dismissing but embracing:
    the too much, the not enough, the mystery of Now.

O Breath of Fire,
We are charged with fire to lie down in Fire.
Not removed but all in,
not dismissive but embracive
that we might experience the revelation—
of You moving and compelling us,
of the full immersion in the Flowing Fire,
of the flames of passion and compassion.
Amen

Prayer of Transformation

O Beloved Spirit,
So much light around us in which to dance and play.
So much dark around us in which to dream and ponder.
So much color abounds in the smallest particles
of the smallest petal of a tropical flower.
So much mystery in the universe enfolds us in, a mystery of
what we don't even know we don't know.

At times, we look at death as so final,
and despair of outrunning its shadow.
Our death so distant until the death of one so near.
Such a short run for us in this light, this dark,
this color, this transparency.
When choked with fear and sorrow,
when beleaguered and battle weary,
when we are ready to concede and say, "Enough!"
remind us that there is
so much light around us in which to dance and play,
so much dark around us in which to dream and ponder,
so much mystery in the universe enfolds us within
what we don't even know we don't know.

We feel You in us like the leaven in the dough
and know You to be that which makes us rise,
to be that which transforms these mysteries, somehow,
into sustenance for the soul, into the bread of life.

For so much color abounds in the smallest particles
of the smallest petal of a tropical flower;
so much mystery in the universe enfolds us within
what we don't even know we don't know
and transforms us into vital sustenance for each other.
Let us embrace this light, this dark,
this color, this transparency,
so that the fullness of our life
enfolds the mystery of the fullness of our death.
Amen

Prayer for a Fortune of Embers

O Beloved Spirit,
We look not for a fortune of gold—
but for embers of insight.

We look not for a wealth of things—
but for sparks of intuition.

We look not for a treasure of money--
but for flames of the imaginative.

Amen

Prayer to the Hallowing of the Temple

O Beloved Spirit,
Hallowed be Thy presence in this temple of ours,
veined in blood, fired by breath
and held together by remnants of stars.

Hallowed be Thy presence in this temple of ours,
the chambers of our hearts
rejuvenate the lifeblood that fills our days
with beauty, with imagination, with love.

Hallowed be Thy presence in this temple of ours,
our essence infused with a holy breath
that travels throughout our far reaches
and brings to fruition a full disclosure of the Divine,
a full immersion into the mystery.

Hallowed be Thy presence in this temple of ours,
latent in the rod,
sealed in the shoot,
secreted in the stave,
expectant with buds and blossoms and ripe almonds.

Hallowed be Thy presence in this temple of ours,
veined in blood, fired by breath
and held together by remnants of stars.

May we call forth the stars inherent in our matter.
May we call forth the buds and blossoms and ripe almonds
integral to our priestly calling.
May we recall that we are more than what we do;
we are manifestations, revelations, epiphanies.
Hallowed be Thy presence in this temple of ours.
Amen

Prayer for Clear Passage

O Beloved Spirit,
Through the Yang in us,
we partake of a communion of fire
that burns within to create without.

Within, we seek the aspiring
that we might create without
despite and because of our not-knowing.

Create in us a clean heart
that the flame may not falter amidst our turmoil.
Create in us a clean mind
that the flame may not be misdirected by what we know.

Through the Yang in us,
we partake of a communion of fire
that burns within to create without.
May all that is Yang in us
find clear passage to create.

Amen

Prayer to Circulating the Fire

O Beloved Spirit,
O Holy Fire, your flame is alive in the breath of us
and upon the intake we feel the *Imago Dei*
circulate through us in imagination, in inspiration, in love.
We articulate Your inter-coursing flame;
it fills us with a light we cannot hide.
You are the breath by which we are quickened into life.
We are made alive through Your fire in us.

O Holy Fire, your flame is alive in the breath of us
and upon the intake we feel the *Imago Dei*
circulate through us in imagination, in inspiration, in love.
Our vessels for Your spirit are not forever;
so short this dance we have with You.
Let us ignite into our fullness—
our one effulgent chance to be,
our one radiant chance to become into being.

O Holy Fire, your flame is alive in the breath of us
and upon the intake we feel the *Imago Dei*
circulate through us in imagination, in inspiration, in love.
Inspire us with a fire
that cannot be quenched, nor squelched, nor squandered.
Inspire us with a fire
that will not settle for being merely people.
Ignite our flame that we may burn
as one flame with Your fire.

O Holy Fire, your flame is alive in the breath of us
and upon the intake we feel the *Imago Dei*
circulate through us in imagination, in inspiration, in love.
Amen

Prayer on the Path of Flames

O Beloved Spirit,
On the path of fire,
the realization of charred remains.

On the path of fire,
an awakening to the flames within.

On the path of fire,
a combustion of joy to be alive just one day more.
Amen

Prayer of Unceasing Prayer

O Beloved Spirit,
Your spirit is made alive in us
not through our sense of unworthiness
or through an appeasement by our good deeds
but through an awakened imagination—
a full, intercoursing flow of our *mater* and our star.

At times, our prayers are in fragments,
chopped into corners of time
where we fight to stave off the invaders.
Instead, may we find ourselves in unceasing prayer
though there be endless invasions of
too much to consider and too much to repair.

At times, our prayers are in fragments
chopped into bits of wishes and wants.
Instead, may we find ourselves in unceasing prayer,
where the valves of our heart flow unconstricted
and we are living in full communion.

At times, our prayers are in fragments,
chopped into categories for special occasions.
Instead may we find ourselves in unceasing prayer,
moving from the light of the inner
though the outer be darkened with the constantly cluttered.

At times, our days are such
that there is no time to take for prayer.
Our only hope—to be in unceasing prayer,
to be mixing the *mater* of what we must do
with the star of what is possible,
and in that balance, though all else be askew,
a renewal of Spirit, holy.

Teach us the unceasing prayer, O Beloved Spirit.
Teach us an awakened imagination.

Amen

Prayer for Lines of Yang

O Beloved Spirit,
We call upon the strong, unbroken lines of the creative
and invoke the essence of the dragon,
of fire to reawaken the *origo*
that we may be imaginatively shaped and formed
into our true, specific nature.

Connect us to our lines of lineage, to the Yang,
to the purity of our beginning
that our unnamed essence will reinvigorate
the experience of the name we now wear.

Connect us to our lines of lineage, to the Yang,
to the primal sources of wisdom and right action
that we clearly, cleanly connect what we do with who we are.

Connect us to our lines lineage, to the Yang
that we may become charged with the invigorating joy
of being alive, of being in body, of being generative.

Connect us to our lines of lineage, to the Yang,
that we may make active what is potent within us,
that we may make actual what is potential around us.

Connect us to our lines of lineage, to the Yang,
and embolden us to abandon our fears,
our hesitation to shine, our reticence to burn with fire.

Connect us to our lines of lineage, to the Yang,
that we may take on the arousing force of thunder
and be fully charged with the focus of right decision.

We call upon the strong, unbroken lines of the creative
and invoke the essence of the dragon,
of fire to reawaken the *origo*
that we may be imaginatively shaped and formed
into our true, specific nature.

Amen

Prayer for the Male

O Beloved Spirit,
While we wear a body
either male or female,
we know that within this outer body,
we are both.
And though our particular outer
seems to separate us from the other,
we seek in the inner
a balance of the both.

This day we pray for fire
that it may flare atop our water
in its dance of light and heat.
May its flame fuel us with beauty
as we look for beauty
in all we touch
and in all we create.

Generate and temper in us a flame,
that what is male
will direct us toward what is active,
toward what will activate.
We delight in the light of what is male.
May we cultivate this delight
as we raise the both to a more perfect balance.

Amen

Yin

The goddess is red with the fire of life;
the earth, the solar system,
the galaxy of far-extending space,
all swell within her womb.
For she is the world creatrix,
every mother, ever virgin.
She encompasses the encompassing,
nourishes the nourishing,
and is the life of everything that lives.

Joseph Campbell

Prayer of Yin

O Beloved Spirit,
Earth above, earth below. K'un over K'un.
Three broken lines over three broken lines:
the Chinese hexagram for Yin or the receptive.
Its attribute, devotion; its image, earth.
Yin, the receptive—the perfect complement to Yang, the creative.
Its power, in devotion; its glory, through reception.
The creative initiates; the receptive gives birth.
Three broken lines above. *Hear our prayer, O God.*
Three broken lines below. *Use us. Use us. Use us.*
K'un above, an asking in. K'un below, a response of service.

Six broken lines form a central channel
that makes way for the creative.
And so we invoke the power of the female
whose canal gives passage to the seed, and birth to the Son.
And so we invoke the power of the female
as we wait in the upper room.
As we wait, we still the mind and hush the chatter of the day
and serve as a chalice to the rushing wind.
And our cup overflows.
And tongues of fire guide our words
through languages we do not know.
And the mystery is not in what we generate
but in what enters us from outside of our understanding
and mixes with the inside of our desire to receive.
And through this invocation—new wine,
new words, new birth, new spirit.
Three broken lines above. *Hear our prayer, O God.*
Three broken lines below. *Use us. Use us. Use us.*
K'un above—an asking in. K'un below—a response of service.

O Beloved Spirit,
Pair our need to be still, to listen, to receive
with our longing to be more, to create, to achieve.
Teach us the three broken lines above,
placed over the three broken lines below
that we may channel the earth of us and give birth to the best of us.
Amen

Prayer for Release

O Beloved Spirit,
From this the grip of fear,
from this grip of inadequacy,
from this grip of impatience,
from this grip of unfairness, release us.

In this release,
reopen the cooling waters of our hearts,
the untainted waters sourced deep in our beginnings.
In this release,
reopen the clear, clean channels of frolic and play
and let our hearts dance this day.
In this release,
reopen the joyous murmuring of an unceasing flow
that enthuses our heart
and courses through these veins of ours.

You have hidden us in the protective darkness of the womb.
You have confined us to this tiny hut
of what we think we know.
And yet, You have teased us with this inescapable sense of
the more, the yes, the unknowable.
How fearsome!
How awesome!
How slow we are to see.
How unfair it seems to be so unreachable.

From this the grip of fear,
from this grip of inadequacy,
from this grip of impatience,
from this grip of unfairness, release us.

In this release reopen us, reconnect us,
renew our wellspring, replenish and resupply us.
Let us resound with the shushing sounds of clear waters
and from these hushes—untainted listening.

Amen

Prayer for the Expression

O Beloved Spirit,
Alive in the mystery of birth,
alive in the mystery of death,
we look for ways to give expression
to the love implanted in our hearts.
As we wake and as we sleep, we carry into each dream, our desire.
Escalate this desire into a passion full-flowered—
blooming light on our right hand and light on our left hand,
blooming light above us and light beneath us.

Alive in the mystery of birth;
alive in the mystery of death,
we look for ways to give expression
to the love implanted in our hearts.
Through touch and scent and taste,
let us circulate this love through one another.
Through moments of the Small and moments of the Great,
let us circulate this love through one another.
Through moments of music and dance
and poetry and art and worship,
let us circulate this love through one another.
Through times of joy and times of sorrow,
through times of discouragement and times of achievement,
let us circulate this love through one another.

And in this our dance of life,
escalate our desire into a passion full-flowered—
blooming light on our right hand and light on our left hand,
blooming light above us and light beneath us.
Let us give expression to the love implanted in our hearts
becoming at one with all that is Human
and with all that is Divine,
all believed and all beloved.

Amen

Prayer for Purification

O Beloved Spirit,
Impatient with the way things turn out,
I try so hard but it's still not enough.
I want to strike rocks and bring forth water.
I want to call down manna on a wilderness of disappointment.
I want to throw down my staff so it jolts into a snake.

Disenchanted with my own overlay of optimism,
I fold my arms and I do not want to pray.
Frustrated with the negative backwash despite my good intentions,
I fold my arms and I do not want to pray.
Maddened that I try so hard and it's still not enough,
I fold my arms and I do not want to pray.

I think, O Beloved Spirit, this is when I most need to pray.
Instead of petulance, teach me to pray—
open arms, detached from the outcome.
Instead of indignation, teach me to pray—
open arms, detached from the outcome.
Instead of despair, teach me to pray—
open arms, detached from the outcome.

Teach me to pray,
unfolding my arms and detaching from the outcome.
And in this hallowedness, my way of becoming prayer—
of unfolding my arms
and letting emerge what is in play
rather than overlaying what I want it to be.
Into Your hands, I commend the results.
Teach me to pray.

Amen

Prayer for the Heart of the Heart

O Beloved Spirit,
Heart of our heart, breath of our breath,
all nourishing source:
bathe us in the Beloving,
refresh us in quiet waters,
restore us in pastures green.
Out of the center of our center,
holy bones, sacred music, canvases of color.
Be not thou far off.

Into You we will pour our spirits
when this shell of ours is used up;
pour into us Now.
Into You we will pour our spirit
when all our inner wranglings cease;
pour into us Now.
Into You we will pour our spirit
when all prayers have stopped murmuring;
pour into us Now.
Can we learn to be so filled with You
that when we spill out of this body and into the next,
we will not even notice?
Can we so love and be-loved
that we can't say when our waters merge into Yours
and Your waters into ours?
Can we ever be so empty that we will never be so full?

O Beloved Spirit,
heart of our heart, breath of our breath,
all nourishing source:
bathe us in the Beloving,
refresh us in quiet waters,
restore us in pastures green.
Out of the center of our center,
holy bones, sacred music, canvases of color.
Be not thou far off.

Amen

Prayer for Free

O Beloved Spirit,
Lead us to the cave, O Lord.
Let it swallow us into its darkness,
no sound deafening our ears,
no view overwhelming our eyes.
In the wealth of its nothingness, teach us free.

Free to hear
without the distortion of our opinions.
Free to be led
without the distraction of where others have gone.
Free to be silent
without the guilt of a goal.
Free to be wise
without the trap of an explanation.

Seal us off that we might be unsealed.
Confine us that we might be unbounded.
In the darkest dark
where all is lost,
teach us free.

Amen

Prayer for Keeping Clear

O Beloved Spirit,
The heavens empty out their heaviness in torrents of rain
and the way roars in the rush of roiling waters
dislodging upstream debris and sediment.
And the force of water surges as it collects
more and more rivulets that flow in tangles down the slopes,
amping up the volume and the speed of the flash.
Can the way sustain such an onslaught?

O Beloved Spirit, help us to keep clear our culverts, our conduits.
Help us sustain a way to channel
the madness, the discontent, the disturbing.
While we cannot control the rains, the "when" and the "how much",
we can control keeping the way clear.

O Beloved Spirit, sometimes we try too hard;
sometimes not hard enough.
Sometimes we speak before we have found our truth;
sometimes we hold on to a hard silence like a weapon.
Sometimes we are rash and unthinking;
sometimes we are slow to act in our overthinking.
Too often, we get in the way of the way
and the mounting debris constricts free passage.

Grace us with remorse
that we will not harden into our sense of rightness.
Grace us with forgiveness
that we will not be preoccupied with a self-stinging.
Grace us with vision
that we will revitalize with seeing our way clear.
Grace us with lightness of being.
that we will not succumb to heaviness of spirit.
Grace us with love
that we can embrace and sustain the torrent;
that we can embrace and sustain the moment;
that we can embrace and sustain the way of our way.

Amen

Prayer to Be Nourishment

O Beloved Spirit,
Deep down and rooted in the ancestral code of me—
the longing for You, my beloved.
Deep down and rooted in this habitation of spirit—
the longing for You, my beloved.
Deep down and rooted into the far reaches
of time's infinite spiral—
the longing for You, my beloved.

And how do I reach You except upon my altar?
And how do I join You except through Your fire?
And how do I mix into You except through the dissolution
of that which I am most attached; except through the dissolution
of what secures me most; except through the dissolution
of what I think most makes me unique?

And how do I reach You except upon my altar?
And how do I join You except through Your fire?
Must it be by way of smoke and flame through my own ashes?
It must be. It must be.

Un-join what binds my life now
that I may enjoin Your life unbounded.
And how do I reach You except upon my altar?
And how do I join You except through Your fire?
Though it be by way of smoke and flame,
through my own ashes,
release this visceral longing now
that I may in spirit reunite as One.

And how do I reach You except upon my altar?
And how do I join You except through Your fire?
Though it be by way of smoke and flame;
through my own ashes,
unmake what I offer now upon my altar
that I may be remade into acceptable nourishment for You.
Amen

Prayer to Place

O Beloved Spirit,
In the lush timbers of Your love,
awake with the fresh smells of a rain-endowed earth,
so much green is crowding
beneath the encircling limbs of the forest
seeking its place in the sun.

Where is our place in this melding mixture
of so much color and song
and dance of life consuming life to sustain life?

Where is our place in this universe
of the unbounded bursts of stars and collections of galaxies
and shimmering icy rings wrapped around planetary orbs
so many millions of light years beyond?

We know our days to be labored with the "much-to-dos."
And we know our to-dos so often
to be daunting or to be tedious
or to distract us from full participation with the dance.

Let us remember and remember and remember
our place, our calling,
to carry into the life we have been given
the rapture of Your breath
and to imbue the hollow of the moment
with the fire of Your hallowed inspiration,
Your hallowed expiration.

O Beloved Spirit, let us not lose our place in this place
but in all we do or try to do or want to do
let us remember and remember and remember
that we are called to be an organ of joy
and let us pipe into this life we lead
Your full-throated, breath-endowed song of joy,
ever re-sounding joy.

Amen

Prayer Beyond the Next

O Beloved Spirit,
I am in a bottleneck of nexts—
    the next job to do
    the next thought to write
    the next thing to say
and everything is juxtaposed
against what comes next.
In this succession of nexts,
I need a next of no thing,
a next of what cannot be classified or catalogued or booked,
a next of no thing, wholly other than thing
and name and known.

I am in a congestion of nexts—
    the next door,
    the next possibility,
    the next challenge
and cannot clear the way.

Beyond the seemingly ceaseless nexts of my days,
intersect my here with Your always.
Pray through me that I may know how to pray.
Love through me that I may know how to love.
Give through me that I may know how to give.
Hear my prayer.
Hollow out the clutter of the next
that I may hallow the impetus of the now.
Amen

Prayer for the Intersection

O Beloved Spirit,
Breathe into this moment—
that in the union of breath and inspiration—
our one chance to be like no other.

Amen

Prayer for the Female

O Beloved Spirit,
While we wear a body
either male or female,
we know that within this outer body,
we are both.
And though our particular outer
seems to separate us from the other,
we seek in the inner
a balance of both.

This day we pray for earth
that it may flower into place
and be hearth to the fire—
a civilizing form to the passion.
And in our devotion,
nourishment for the root of us,
nourishment for the soul of us.

Hold and behold in us rich earth,
that what is female
will give form to what is genius,
to what is *origo*.
We delight in the substance,
the essence of what is female.
May we cultivate this delight
as we raise the both to a more perfect balance.

Amen

God

Inasmuch as He is the creator,
God is triune and one,
but as infinity, He is neither triune nor one,
nor anything else that one can say.
For the names attributed to God
are derived from creatures;
in Himself, God is ineffable
and above all that one can name or say.

Nicholas of Cusa

Prayer of God

O Beloved Spirit,
So, here we are in the midst of this most Holy of Holies.
Our birth—a baptism into beholding and being held—
an immersion into the mystery of being alive, awake, being human.
Our baptism—a birth into seeing and being seen—
an immersion into the mystery of being transformed,
being reawakened, being human.
Our birth and our baptism—all about being and becoming being—
our immersion into joy, into the marvelous, into the terrifying,
into the unfathomable beauty and into the unknowable darkness.

So, here we are in the midst of this most Holy of Holies.
A vibrating discourse of wings and songs.
An intoxicating drink of mountains and stars.
A charged exchange of loving and being loved.
So, here we are in the midst of this most Holy of Holies.
So finite but full of the eternal.
So small but bursting with immensity.
So limited but transformed by the limitless.
So, here we are in the midst of this most Holy of Holies.

So, here we are in the midst of this most Holy of Holies.
May we be the infoldings of Your voice
vibrating into song as we inhale you,
carrying into our incarnation this one chance—Your inspiration.
May we resonate Your beloving,
amplify the oscillating playfulness of Your creation
as it resounds throughout the labyrinth of this—our only moment.
May we be the receptors for Your touch,
enlivening every cell with a rush of generative pleasure—
a sense of the sacrum as we walk uprightly—our one chance.

So, here we are in the midst of this most Holy of Holies.
Our birth—a baptism into beholding and being held.
Our baptism—a birth into seeing and being seen.
Our birth and our baptism all about being and becoming being.
Amen

Prayer to Be the Holy Breath

O Beloved Spirit,
May we circulate a breath that revitalizes our love.
May we circulate a breath that revitalizes our joy.
May we circulate a breath that revitalizes our creative energy.
O Holy Breath, circulate in all Your fullness through us.

And though it seems we are the one
who stops and starts and holds the breath,
may we realize it is the breath
that stops and starts and holds us.
And though it seems we do the breathing,
may we submit to being breathed by You.
And though it seems we are the one who inspires,
may we realize that we are the inspired.

Upon Your breath, may we articulate a song inspired.
Upon Your breath, may we exhale all despair.
Upon Your breath, may we articulate a thought inspired.
Upon Your breath, may we exhale all apathy.
Upon Your breath, may we articulate a prayer inspired.
Upon Your breath, may we exhale all fear.
O Holy Breath, articulate and exhale
in all Your fullness through us.

Amen

Prayer for the Wholeness of the Seed

O Beloved Spirit,
What is the geometry of the seed
that inherent in its shape
is the towering sequoia
or the flowering magnolia
or the fruit of the mango?
What is the algebra of the seed
that so necessitates an expression
of vibrant petals
or fragrant scents
or sweet tastes?
And if I am but a husk to Your seed,
what is the geometry, the algebra,
of You in me?

I am distracted.
The noise seeps through
even my most quiet of moments
and disturbs my sleep.
Hold me in Your heart
that I might contain You in mine.
Be the spark to my spark
that I might be alight with You.
And though the increments of time
seem to fragment my days,
bring me closer to the wholeness of the seed.
That what is without fragments, without increments,
will take shape, will find expression in me.

Amen

Prayer for Beloving

O Beloved Spirit,
So much thinking, doubting and wanting
diverts us from our Here,
sidetracking us with what we wish we had done
or what we think might happen.

We have an image of You as an inexhaustible fire
that fuels, does not consume.
This image (probably no more accurate
than our childhood image of a bearded old man
folded in clouds sitting on a throne of judgment)
brings us no closer to knowing the unknowable,
and we cannot think it through,
but at least approaches how active
and activating You are in our lives.

While Your laws may enlighten,
it is Your animating breath that delights.
Through it, though distracted, we are replenished.
Through it, though hesitant, we are made alive.
Through it, though scattered, we are made whole.

Keep us close to our need, our doubt,
that we move beyond our be-thinking
and find the inner-most ground,
through our beholding of the mystery,
through our beloving of Your presence in our Here.
Amen

Prayer for the Radiance of the Moment

O Beloved Spirit,
For this radiance that animates this day,
and heightens the greens of this earth,
and brightens most brilliantly the blues of this sky,
and casts an iridescence in its play of light across this land,
we are grateful.

For this radiance that moves us to adore you,
that delights us with its charge of ever-generative fire,
that undulates through the landscape in its alchemy of heat,
re-creating the creation in rhythms of sun and moon,
in seasons birthing seasons-next,
we are grateful.

For the inner radiance that animates this soul of ours,
and fills our hearts with the deep-seated sense of joy,
and lights us up with the pleasure of an ahhh and an ah-ha,
and wakens our minds to a spontaneous response of love,
and freely circulates through us in a glow of God,
we are grateful.

And though our time is short,
we are permeated with the Eternal
in the radiance of this moment;
and though our days are dogged with
more than we can get done at any given time,
it is Your radiance
that transfigures our time into the timeless.
And though we go about being as busy as we know to be,
it is this treasure of the timeless which fills all our days.

For this, we are grateful.
All believed and all beloved.

Amen

Prayer to Be Occupied

O Beloved Spirit,
O Holy, Hallowed Place, occupy our minds
and let us remember the place from where we came,
and let it intersect with the place we now find ourselves,
and let that intersection of holiness and hallowedness
move us to the place where we are going.

O Holy, Hallowed Place, occupy our hearts
and wash us in vibratory song of wind and birds,
and refresh us in the cleansing rains,
and renew us in the vital greens of forest and meadow.

O Holy, Hallowed Place, occupy our life force, our souls
and reclaim the thoughts weighed down by deadlines,
and infiltrate the depleted feelings wearied from too much,
and fill up every room of us and every corner of us
with a unique sense to guide us beyond sight and beyond hearing,
with a unique sense of the Holy and the Hallowed
embedded in everything we do and see and are.
Occupy us, O Holy, Hallowed Place.

Occupy us, O Holy, Hallowed Breath,
replenish our minds with fragrances of the sublime,
renew our hearts with oxygenating compassion,
recharge our life force, our souls with a breath
so enveloping, so engulfing, so animating
that we are charged with the Holy,
and there are no fleshy borders confining us,
and there are no stultifying labels and preconceptions separating us,
and there are no inhibitions and deprecations minimizing
the Holiness and the Hallowedness of Your Breath
now fully and completely occupying
our minds, our hearts, our life force.

Occupy us, that we may be One.

Amen

Prayer in All Our Unlikeliness

O Beloved Spirit,
Unlike all other times, this time.
Unlike all other places, this place.
In all our unlikeliness, let us see and be seen by You
in full communion with the astounding and the hidden.

Unlike all other breaths, this breath.
Unlike all other inspirations, this inspiration.
In all our unlikeliness, let us hear and be heard by You
in full communion with the music and the silence.

Unlike all other chances, this one chance.
Unlike all other dreams, this one dream.
In all our unlikeliness, let us know and be known by You
in full communion with the unmediated and the unknowable.

Unlike all other loves, this love.
Unlike all other joys, this joy.
In all our unlikeliness, let us love and be loved by You
in full communion with the mystery and the incarnate.

Hear our prayer, O Beloved Spirit,
may we see and be seen, hear and be heard.
Hear our prayer, O Beloved Spirit,
may we know and be known, love and be loved.

Unlike all other universes, this one universe.
Unlike all other planets, this one planet.
Unlike all other prayers, this one prayer we pray.

In all our unlikeliness, our one chance to be.
Amen

Prayer for Jehovah

O Beloved Spirit,
As we project what we know of our many selves
through the experiences we think we want,
we can easily infer the routes we should take
and the qualities we wish we could have
and the things we hope to acquire.
And yet, Jehovah is not in the wind.

As we compare ourselves to the selves down the street
and the selves at our work
and the selves on a page or pictured on a screen,
we can easily impose the fear of a misstep,
an action unfinished, a decision badly made.
And yet, Jehovah is not in the quaking of the earth.

As we collect up words and phrases to hurl
at what we have come to distrust
and gather with like-minded men to arm ourselves against
what makes us angry or sad,
we can easily defend the passion behind the roles we choose.
and yet, Jehovah is not in the fire.

Must it take forty days and forty nights
lodged on a mountain, inside a cave
to learn to recognize You?
To realize You are not in the wind of our wishes,
or in the quake of our fears, or in the fire of our opinions?
Rather, You are deep in the cavern of our One,
the still small voice.

So personal, only our true one can hear it.
So personal, only our true one can respond to it.
So personal, only our true one can evoke from it.
We look for You, Jehovah,
in the small of our days,
in the still of our desires,
in the voice of our *origo,* of the one true self.

Amen

Prayer for Abundance

O Beloved Spirit,
Teach us abundance.
It is not in what we hold
but in what we release.
It is not in what we believe
but in what we cannot know.
It is not in what we acquire
but in what we offer back.

Teach us abundance.
That by embracing our emptiness,
we may be filled with Your fullness.
That in letting go of our holdings,
we may inherit the gift of our potential.
That in the very absence of our answers
we may find the very presence,
Your Spirit, made holy.

Teach us abundance.
Let the light that burned so brightly
through the Christ, the Buddha, the Prophet,
burn brightly through us now in all its passion.
We need nothing but our nothingness
to be filled with Your allness.
In the poverty of our spirit,
we seek the riches of Your kingdom here,
Your kingdom now.

Teach us abundance
that Your kingdom may come,
Here and now—through us.

Amen

Prayer for Fluency

O Beloved Spirit,
Make fluent my tongue
with the unspeakable.
Make fluent my mind
with the unknowable.
Make fluent my heart
with what passes all understanding—
the fire of your love.

Make fluent the light on my tongue.
Make fluent the light of my mind.
Make fluent the light in my heart
that I may be conversant with the Holy.

Make me fluent in the affluence of holy gifts
keeping me in unceasing conversation.
Make me fluent in the unspeakable
that the dialogue of the Word
as it speaks itself into flesh
may continue through me.

Amen

Prayer for the Gift of Being Present

Beloved Spirit,
To the altar of this moment,
we bring the gift of being present:
Here in the in-breath,
Here in the out-breath.
To the altar of this moment,
we bring the gift of being present:
Here in the intentions of our prayer,
Here in the conversations with Spirit.
To the altar of this moment,
we bring the gift of being present:
Here in the emanations of friendship,
Here in the *enthusiasmos* of love.

How rich a moment—
how laden with harvest and seed,
how deep its roots,
how nourishing its fruit,
how marvelous the mystery of being—
of being here,
of being human,
of Being Human intersecting this *Here* with You.

To the altar of this moment,
we bring the gift of our presence:
presence of mind—insight and "ah ha" and "oh my",
presence of heart—intuition and inspiration and tears,
presence of body—sight and sound and taste and smell and touch.
To the altar of this moment,
we burn up the despair, dissipate the dread.

Here at the altar of *Here,* help us to be *Here*—
no scatterings across nagging to-dos,
no stutterings across shoulds and musts.
May we bring the only gift we have to give—our presence—
to the radiant gift You continuously give us—the Present.
Amen

Prayer for the Way

O Beloved Spirit,
To You who has woven Yourself into stone
and sea for years summed into billions,
to You who blazes into stars hung
in galaxies unbounded,
to You who splices spirit with body and mind
that we might reach Human,
we pay homage to the mystery of the way.

And though the mystery be in us, it is also beyond us.
And though it be beyond us, it unfolds through us
into a thousand fruits of grace.

O Beloved Spirit,
let us not abandon this grace
by holding fast to our fear, our discontent, our anger.
Instead, inspire us to be a community of belovers.
Let us become a community that holds fast
to the Way of Your grace—
to the "ah-ha!" of discovery
and to the mystery of being human.

Amen

Quest

Put Your feet down with pollen.
Put your hands down with pollen.
Put your head down with pollen.
Then your feet are pollen;
your hands are pollen;
your body is pollen;
your mind is pollen;
your voice is pollen.
The trail is beautiful.
Be still...

Navajo legend

Prayer for the Journey

O Beloved Spirit,
It is a precarious journey.
There is safety
in affirmations, in labels, in achievements, in recognition,
but there is no safety on the Way.
Affirmations, labels, achievement and recognition
get in the way of the Way
and must be set aside.

While we think of it as
"the straight and narrow path,"
really it is a swirling spiral.
We come around to almost the same place
with almost the same insight,
only one loop in, one layer deeper.

Take us one loop in,
one layer deeper,
that we may leave where we are behind,
until we cycle 'round again
and find that where we've been
is in tandem with where we will be.

So in between the tension
of the outer swirl and the inner swirl
is the point of our arriving departure.

Take us
one loop in,
one layer deeper,
where we are always at the point of our between.
Amen

Prayer for the Leaving

O Beloved Spirit,
Destinations call us to embark.
Returns call us to transform.
Departures call us to arrive fully present.
Gather up these blessings and let them nourish the light.
Gather up these inspirations and let them nourish the flame.
Gather up these invocations and let them nourish the spirit.

Remind us that in the adventure, we go in love.
Remind us that in the difficulties, we go in love.
Remind us that in the joyous, we go in love.
Gather up these blessings and let them nourish the light.
Gather up these inspirations and let them nourish the flame.
Gather up these invocations and let them nourish the spirit.

In the letting go of place, a new and renewed place.
In the letting go of home, a new and renewed home.
In the letting go of what has held us here in the moment,
a beholding of what is new and renewed in the Always.
Gather up these blessings and let them nourish the light.
Gather up these inspirations and let them nourish the flame.
Gather up these invocations and let them nourish the spirit.
Amen

Prayer to Be of the Plan

O Beloved Spirit,
Align us to your outpouring
that we may be a channel to your fire.
Like blood, infuse us with your life
that what flows from us
is from your fire flowing through us.
Attune us to your phrasing,
Your pattern for the breath,
that what sounds forth through our choices
is the sound of a daily matins, a nightly vespers.

How easy to think that what we want is what we need
and that by forcing what we want,
we can become all that we are.
Be at work in us
as we work to renounce that which attaches us.
Be at work in us
that our will may be your will,
that our work may be your work,
that your plan may unfold in part through our all.
Amen

Prayer to Further Union

O Beloved Spirit,
We have heard it said by our poets and prophets that
"Old men ought to be explorers."
We have heard it said that "Here and there does not matter."
And they have directed us with this admonition,
"We must be still and still moving into another intensity
for a further union, a deeper communion."

And if it is true that in our end is our beginning,
may we embark on this quest into the Still
as we end where we have been,
and begin where we have ended.
And may we find ourselves totally present
in the gift of the Still in this Present.

Beloved Spirit, may we be ever-curious,
masters of great questions, explorers of great universes—
not just sightseers dashing from one marvel to the next,
but deep sea divers exhuming treasures hidden,
uncovering gems long lost to us,
not just tourists skimming the readily accessible,
but deep-space pioneers
discovering stars hitherto unknown to us.

On this day, may new birth be made known to us.
May we name it and lay claim to it as our own.
May we embrace its cries and hold it dear to our hearts
and immerse ourselves in the intensity
of this further union, of this deeper communion
now gracing us with regenerative life and love
as it calls us into the "still moving into" a magnificent moment.

Beloved Spirit, may we be ever curious,
masters of great questions, explorers of great universes—
still moving into another intensity
for a further union, a deeper communion.

Amen

Prayer for the Great Lack

O Beloved Spirit,
Great oceans of ignorance
define the shores of what I have discovered to be true.
Great seas of uncertainty
push against the landscape of what I trust.
Great clouds of unknowing
crowd the far horizon and seal me from bright answers.

Through dangers and difficulties,
my great lack.
Through decisions and changes,
my great lack.
Through deaths and disappointments,
my great lack.

Curious that my one foothold
amid these waters—
my great lack.
For in my lack,
the very place I most find Your grace to be.

For where I am empty in assurances,
You fill me with hope.
Where I am empty in answers,
You bring surprise.
Where I lack knowledge,
You provide imagination.

Take my great lack and use it
as if it were a lamp for Your light:
light of hope, surprise, imagination.

Amen

Prayer of Reassurances

O Beloved Spirit,
a gully wash of a week
where it rained the unexpected for days,
and I thought I'd never be able
to stay afloat.
And yet,
I never felt abandoned,
only tested and tried.

A gully wash of a week
where the clouds kept rushing over the mountains
and pouring onto the open spaces
forcing me to decide
before I had time to think.
And yet,
I never felt forsaken,
only shaken and shook.

A gully wash of a week
where the seeming letup
was just a segue into an even bigger squall
and I thought I'd never regain my footing
on the water-logged ground.
And yet,
I never felt dislodged,
only on call and on alert.

And though the week was awash
with too much all at once,
I always knew the presence of Your love
and felt a steadfast stirring of love towards You.
Amen

Prayer for Help, for Strength

O Beloved Spirit,
In our times of sickness,
in our times of impasse,
in our times of loneliness,
where is our help, our strength?

In our times where we no longer feel safe,
where we no longer carry the assurance of goodness,
where we no longer see what once seemed clear,
where is our help, our strength?

In our times when we feel overshadowed by another,
when we feel powerless to change what we want to change,
when we feel impoverished to do what we hope to do,
where is our help, our strength?

We sleep, but cannot rest in our dreams.
We work, but cannot find nourishment in our achievements.
We pray but then worry over our own words
and fuss with the silent reply.
Where is our help? Where is our strength?

Because we are beset on every side
by the unsettling pace of change in our lives,
we wish for intervention that all will be righted
and what is right will be secured.
How tempting it is for us to let go of our quest
in exchange for being sure, for knowing without a doubt.
Anchor us in the experience of a spirit
higher than our doubting mind, deeper than our hurting heart.
Help us, in our times of need, and
in our times when we think we no longer need to submit—
to Your spirit with us, to Your spirit in us, to Your spirit through us.
That we will rise to the call of this adventure called life
and through Your spirit find our help and our strength.
Amen

Prayer for Emptiness

O Beloved Spirit,
In all our doings,
we question should we
and can we do more?
And yet, "more" is an ever-sliding scale—
like the horizon—always just out of reach.
There is no rescue in more,
only recrimination.

In all our doings,
we wonder if less would be enough.
And yet, less is fraught with doing the right thing only
and that sense of right is shifting ground—
shadowed with its border of doubt.
There's no safety in less,
only more judgment.

In all our doings, then,
it is not finding more or doing less,
but in filling up with emptiness
that there might be a place for Your fullness.

Let us, in all our doings, undo the attachments.
Let us, in all our doings, undo the holding on.
Let us, in all our doings, undo the need for controlling.
May we, in our emptying out,
experience the freedom of our opening up.
May we, through Your grace and through our emptiness,
fill up with a revitalizing joy in all doings.
Amen

Prayer for Unlikely Places

O Beloved Spirit,
Unlikely places—
our blurting of anger, our experience of fear,
brings us home to the native earth of our soul.
Ironically, the impingement of our pain
grounds our love for the dance.

Unlikely places breach the sterile borders
of our places of comfort,
and thrust our thoughts into play.
Places of "embark" and "challenge"
disturb our walk of sleep
and set us upright on a path of grace.

Unlikely places startle us awake
and combust in an intake of Holy Breath,
where we are inspired to belove more
than we ever believed we could.
Places of dueling words, tension-filled unknowns,
foreign roads marked by foreign signs,
send us forward as we leave behind.

O Beloved Spirit, we are grateful for all the unlikely places
revealed in this great quest of life—
unlikely places that awaken us
to what is most alive and holy,
unlikely places that startle us
with a joy to create and be created anew,
unlikely places that catalyze in us
such surprising transformations.

Amen

Prayer for Realizing the Boon

O Beloved Spirit,
May I not shrink before Your grace and claim,
"Such a worm as I."
Nor scoff in the face of Your gifts with a smug,
"It is not for me to know."
Nor sit in the spring of so much water and say,
"I thirst."
Your bounty, my boon.

I cannot fathom my ignorance
without expanding my knowledge.
I cannot know my smallness
without embracing Your greatness.
I cannot experience my poverty
without the surfeit of Your wealth.
Your bounty, my boon.

I bring to You the humor of my ever expanding limitations.
For, as I claim to know more and more ground,
I discover it to be bordered by a universe
I did not even know was there.
As I push out my limits, I find my limits.
The inexhaustible beauty of Your bounty
brushes up against my shore like an ocean.

And so, it is what I press to know
that reveals how much remains to be known.
And in that bounty of the unknown, of the unknowable, my boon.
Amen

Prayer for Beauty

O Beloved Spirit,
Let beauty have its way with us—
arouse us, awaken us, bless us—
calling us to create, to love, to aspire.

Amen

Prayer for the Rushing Wind

O Beloved Spirit,
In the rushing wind—
a change of seasons,
a casting of seeds,
a modulation of mood and color.
We watch the landscape ripen into hues
of oranges and yellows and russets.
And we delight in the play of leaves set on fire and
in the frenzy of squirrels as they scold and store up their supply.

In the rushing wind—
a change of seasons,
a casting of seeds
an upper room punctuated with tongues of fire.
And in this rushing wind, we experience
a language of inspiration
of beloving,
a language for the mind of the heart.

In the rushing wind—
our change of season,
our time to cast seeds,
our time to be filled with Your breath—
as if You are breathing us,
as if You are articulating through us a new song.
In the rushing wind—
a new inspiration,
a new song—
it is in us and of us
and we are in the rushing wind of Spirit.

Amen

Home

Father, we are so long in this wilderness of noise.
Help us not to weary
picking up manna, moving the tents,
setting up the tabernacle,
first one place, then another.
Help us to be constant in our service,
pushing out noise, letting in music
holding back darkness, bringing in light.
Lead us home, Father.
It can be anywhere; it must be somewhere.
We tire of wandering,
long for the promised land.
Yet, not one of us would press a claim
if we could but know the fruits
are for our children to taste.
Father, bless us, as we pick up manna, move the tents.

Teri Martin

Prayer of Harvest Home

O Beloved Spirit,
Burnt leaves, spent trees, the golds have crisped into browns
and November engulfs us with its encroaching darkness.
All the world whispers "go in, settle in, be at home with the inner."
We are grateful for the time to take in the harvest,
store up the earth's goodness, gather in the fruits of hard labor,
as the days tuck-in early and the earth slips into a deep sleep.
We welcome in this season of in-gathering,
and are grateful for the time we are given
to enumerate the gratefulness for our givens,
the gifts of home and harvest.

For soulful friends true through the many years,
for the light in young faces as they explore the amazing,
for the smells of dark spices – cinnamon and cloves,
nutmeg and cardamom,
for the healing prayers that reach the root of us,
for skies graced with galaxies of stars,
for our own moon poised among the bright planets,
for a chance to be and to become, for tables spread and glasses filled,
for books to en-trance and dance with our imaginations,
for poems that carry us to our very edges,
for those who have taught us how to love, for those who love us,
for those of valor and ethic—rich with talent,
for those heroes most willing to embark,
for the mystery of being human
and the unitive thread of Spirit that connects us as Family.
We welcome in this season of in-gathering.
We are grateful for the time we are given
to enumerate the gratefulness for our givens—
the gifts of home and harvest.

O Beloved Spirit, in-gather us, take us in
and store us up as for another bright season.
For this gift of life and love and the good things of this earth,
we are grateful.

Amen

Prayer for the Altar of the Home

O Beloved Spirit,
Dark waters, violent struggles,
unthinkable sorrows and disappointments
empty like tributaries into the presence of our Here now.
Rough landscapes, rugged passages, and rustic settings
inflected with faith in something more,
link us to the passion of our Before
and connect us to the passion of our Now.

O Beloved Spirit, we are grateful for the mothers and fathers,
of our mothers' mothers and fathers,
and we are grateful for the mothers and fathers
of our fathers' mothers and fathers,
who braved each day with the best they knew to do
and ensured the presence of our Here now.

O Beloved Spirit, let us not forget the altar in our Homes;
the altar of our Homes, the altar of our Soul-bearing Homes.
May we give homage to those who have gone before us—
not just the ancestors gifted to us at our birth
but those ancestors of our rebirth—
teachers and saints and artists
who nourished our vision
and emboldened us to break past the least within us.

O Beloved Spirit, let the altar of our Homes
be center-point to all who enter;
let the altar of our Homes be an *axis mundi* to this troubled time;
let the altar of our Homes be a polestar to the Times to Come.
Accept our gratefulness for the profound mystery of the Home
and for all it has been for us
and for all it can be for those who follow us.

Amen

Prayer for Place

O Beloved Spirit,
Do not let us lose our place,
even though we are moving so quickly with the times.
Our place is garden, atrium, a chapel of the soul.

Do not let us lose our place even though we do not stop running
or ever cease from trying to catch up.
Our place is fertile soil of the soul, seedbeds full of sprouts,
and roots that draw from sacred springs.

Do not let us lose our place,
even though others would have us wish for more,
or have us settle for common ground.
Instead, our place is fountain with brimming water as its voice.
Our place is a replenishment of light
recast, reflected, rethought through the illumination of great minds.

Do not let us lose our place and slip away,
awash with all the noise of change
and too much, and inequity, and in pride.
Instead, our place is altar alight with prayers
for self and for others, alight with emblems of the good,
the true and the beautiful from the ages, and dedicated heart.

Do not let us lose our place
and be dislodged from what is most core to our very core
nor let our hope be splintered nor our faith diluted
nor our love corralled by fear of being naïve.

Do not let us forget or let us slip-slide away
or lose our place of soul.
Instead, secure in us a place comprised of garden, of fire,
of seedbeds, of atrium and of love.

O Beloved Spirit, do not let us lose our place.
Amen

Prayer to the Scent of Life and Roses

O Beloved Spirit,
The scent of roses mixes with the newborn cries,
here, at the beginning of the life cycle.
And the earth—so much the richer.
We are in profound anticipation of the unmistakable essence
we will come to know as this new one connects us
to beginnings past and to beginnings future—
to the Here of this beginning.
And our life here is so much the richer.
For this life, we are grateful.

The scent of roses mixes with the death-laden ashes,
here, at the completion of the lifecycle.
And the earth is so much the richer.
We are in profound remembrance
of the unmistakable essence we knew
and continue to know and hope to know again.
And our life Here is so much the richer.
For this life, we are grateful.

The scent of roses mixes with our prayers,
here, as we struggle to awaken
to the earth and all its riches and all its fragrances.
We are upended with a grace-filled mystery
that takes our breath away with such beauty
that inspires us as if we were the breath, the oxygen
so necessary for bearing light.
And our life here is so much the richer.
For this life, we are grateful.

The scent of roses mixes
with the aromatic essence of these cries, these ashes, these prayers.
In this, our time Here, we bless lives beginning and lives ending,
lives present and lives past. and our life here is so much the richer.
O Beloved Spirit, O Holy God,
for these lives, for this, our life here, we are grateful.
Amen

Prayer in Gratitude for This Service

Beloved Spirit,
We carry into this service the blessings from our homes
and look to enrich this home where we have gathered
for worship and communion.
We carry into this service the insights from our homes
and look to embellish the conversation at this table
with what has been revealed.
We carry into this service the music from our homes
and look to elaborate on the music here
with what captures our joy.

A sacred moment in a sacred space
made holy by our intention to unite in celebration.
A sacred moment in a sacred space
made holy by our prayers of healing and gratitude.
A sacred moment in a sacred space
made holy by our invocation of fire and the fruit of the vine.

With light all around us
and light before us
and light to the right of us
and light to the left of us
and with a burning light for all those who have gone before us,
help us increase this harvest of the Human: light.
Let us be as nourishment to those gathered here.
Let us be as sustenance to those we hold dear.

May we carry from this sacred home—
renewal, refreshment, rejuvenation.
And may we return to our homes
the light we have created.
We are grateful for this light-making moment,
for this table of lights,
for the light-hearted, the light-minded,
for the light of Your Fiery Spirit.

Amen

Prayer at This Table

O Beloved Spirit,
At this table, we are nourished with the imaginative words
that have changed us,
that have challenged us,
that have called us to something better.
At this table, we are nourished with the conversations of Soul
both past and present—
prayers that intersect this moment
with a vitalizing expression of beloving.
At this table, we are nourished with cherished music
that converts breath and memory into melody,
that transforms voice into praise and harmony.
At this table, a feast for Spirit that we might grow strong in Spirit,
that we might grow together in Spirit,
that we might extend Spirit through the intimacy of this table.

At this table, we bring a shared, imaginative vision
of the human made holy, the Christed human.
At this table, we bring an emotive expression of all that is human
and pray for healing, for renewal, for hope
for those for whom we care.
At this table, we bring our amalgam of joy,
our wonder and our disappointment.
May we be re-sourced in the wealth of Spirit
at this table that we might grow strong in Spirit,
that we might grow together in Spirit,
that we might extend Spirit through the intimacy of this table.
Amen

Prayer for the Holy

O Beloved Spirit,
O holy radiant light that spills into our being and
emits Your essence of tones and new song,
amplify through us
and let us be home to the Holy of Your Spirit.

O holy radiant light that intones Your fiery love
throughout the base of our spine
and the hallowed passages of our hearts
and the sacred cells of our minds,
amplify through us
and let us be home to the Holy of Your Spirit.

O holy radiant light that crescendos
in waves of prayerful overtones of longing, of beloving, of uniting,
amplify through us
and let us be home to the Holy of Your Spirit.

And here in the center of this Center
where we meet to commune in community, in prayer, in inspiration,
amplify through us
and let us be home to the Holy of Your Spirit.

And here in the center of this Center
where we are joined in the "one love",
in the unitive verb of all believing and all beloving,
amplify through us
and let us be home to the Holy of Your Spirit.

And here in the center of this Center
where we are growing and nourishing and becoming soul,
both the soul we call our own and the soul we call ours,
amplify through us
and let us be home to the Holy of Your Spirit.

Amen

Prayer to Be a Blessing

O Beloved Spirit,
In this our invocation,
we call You out into our midst
that we might be a blessing
to those we hold in our hearts.

In this our invocation,
we call You down into our midst
that we might be a blessing
to those who are in need of healing.

In this our invocation,
we call You up into our midst
that we might be a blessing
to those who seek You
through the life and love they generate.

In this our invocation,
we call upon You
invoking the above into the below
so that the here and the now
are full of blessing and Your sacred breath.

Amen

Prayer for Thanksgiving

O Beloved Spirit,
In this tradition of Thanksgiving,
paying homage to our origins
and gathering friends into the
bounds and bonds of family,
we are grateful.

In this tradition of Thanksgiving,
meeting in the chapel of the home
and surrounding a table abundant
with the earth's harvest,
we are grateful.

In this tradition of Thanksgiving,
where this community of friends and family fills us
with the inspired fruits of the spirit
and pours through us a light
to light our sacred lights,
we are grateful.

As we have been given
may we give back a thousand-fold.

Amen

Prayer in Memory of

O Beloved Spirit,
Memories take hold of us as
we feel the door open
and then the draft of a loved one's leaving.
We feel the burnt colors
pile atop the tree's shade.
The extremes of night
press more and more upon the day.
The brazen splash of Fall
now moves into contemplative hues
and we find our thoughts on You
and where our where will be when we are gone
and where the where is of those who have gone before.

Translate our love
that it might reach those we can no longer reach
and convey with this prayer
a nourishment they might receive.
Your gift of life — a brazen splash of Fall.
And for its sustaining grace, we are grateful.
And we give thanks for those
whose memories now fill our shade.

Amen

Prayer for the Family

O Beloved Spirit,
May what we do,
may what we invite in,
may the way we challenge each other
serve as nourishment.

Help this family secure the each
and let each secure this family
so that this home may be a place of nourishment,
a place where we grow in our experience of love,
our understanding of right action,
our testing of will.

Such a short time together, O Beloved Spirit.
May this be a time of building up reserves
from which we can draw strength,
vision, courage, nourishment.

Amen

Prayer to Home in on Home

O Beloved Spirit,
From out of our joy, our enjoyment, our delight,
let us home in on Home and what secures us.
From out of our wonder, our fascination, our breakthroughs
let us home in on Home and what embraces us.
From out of our insights, our revelations, our intuitions,
let us home in on Home and what fortifies us.

Our Home is in the imaginative where our souls are fed
by what is possible, by what is paradoxical, by what is magical.
Our Home is in gratefulness where our hearts are nourished
by kindnesses remembered, by sacred times hallowed.
Our Home is in communion where our spirits are made alive again
by the bread of compassion, by the cup of empathy.

From out of our distress, our angst, our discontent,
let us home in on Home and what secures us.
From out of our frustration, our disappointment, our stress,
let us home in on Home and what embraces us.
From out of our anger, our grief, our sorrow
let us home in on Home and what fortifies us.

Our Home is in the beloving where our souls are fed
by an intimate understanding, by a cleansing of tears.
Our Home is in the remembrances where are hearts are nourished
by memories of friends, of times cherished, of teachers revered.
Our Home is in the holy where our spirits are made alive again
through the uncanny, through the *Imago Dei* revealed in
galaxies of stars and mangers of the human heart.

Let us home in on Home and gather in the harvest of the Spirit:
our love, our joy, our peace, our forbearance, our kindness,
our goodness, our faithfulness, our gentleness and our self-control.
From these, we will be rich enough and have no more to desire.
From these, our Home, our source of nourishment, our source of
inspiration, our secure place from which to unfold and expand.
Amen

Birth and Rebirth

Signs are taken from wonders.
"We would see a sign!"
The word within a word,
unable to speak a word,
swaddled with darkness.
In the juvenescence of the years
came Christ the tiger
to be eaten, to be divided,
to be drunk among whispers.

T.S. Eliot

Prayer for Advent

O Beloved Spirit,
In the mystery of this Advent, this expectant time,
we resound with the joy in the coming birth—the new song.

In the trough of the animal, a spark of the divine child
seeded into the human experience.
Are we so seeded and expectant
with this same bloom of the Divine?

In the *chronos* of swaddling clothes,
a new birth infused with the *kairos* of Holy Spirit.
Can it be? Can we re-incarnate this birth?

In the mystery of this Advent, this expectant time,
we resound with the joy in the coming birth—the new song.
In the midst of the watch and the necessities of the flock,
a new song full of myth and madness and imaginativeness.
Can we be so smitten that we will forever change and be changed
because of its uncontestable beauty?

The days only seem to march forward
as they are squeezed tighter and tighter by the shortness of light.
In our frozen darkness,
we are taken in by the mystery of the star
infolding and unfolding, inverting and everting,
diving deeper, aspiring higher—
the human steeped in divine disclosure.

And we experience first-hand an irrational timelessness,
yielding unexpected moments of grace—
yields of friendship, of worship, of kinship,
yields of insight, of music, of poetry,
yields of laughter, of tears, of awe-filled wonder.

In the mystery of this advent, this expectant time,
we resound with the joy in the coming birth—the new song.
Amen

Prayer in Gratefulness for the Star in Our Advent

O Beloved Spirit,
Here we are again, in a cycle of time, in a season of advent,
in these days of an encroaching darkness, and yet a star.
So many fiddly bits, so many pieces and parts,
so many scatterings of dreams and hopes, and yet a mystery.
So long the journey, so pressed with the impending,
so labored with the next thing,
so dogged with the undone, and yet a birth.

In this Advent season that comes in a wave of contractions
and a squeezing tight of the daylight,
let us be attentive to the star,
awake to the mystery,
alert to the birth.

May deep December nights remind us
that the gift of birth is inside us
as well as all around us.
So much life waiting to be named
and unfold through us and around us.

Accept our gratefulness for the star, the mystery, the birth,
hidden in the darkness of the "not enough."
Accept our gratefulness for the star, the mystery, the birth,
hidden in the darkness of the "too much."
Accept our gratefulness for the star, the mystery, the birth,
renewed in this season, this cycle of time.

How rich the mystery of being Human,
how bright the chance to birth a star.

Amen

Prayer for Abandonment

O Beloved Spirit,
The harvest quits.
The days shorten.
The nights darken.
And all we want
is to be tucked in with reassurances.

Wars and rumors of wars rumble.
The fear of not enough
quickens and fuels our once quieted fears.
With the world so raw, so close to the edge,
where is our refuge but in desperation?

Hear us in our abandonment,
as we descend into the darkest dark.
We grieve the loss of what was so familiar to us.
How is it that this darkness
heralds the season of the Christ,
the season to be born?

Help us in our abandonment,
to despair of all save abandonment alone.
For it alone, as it did for the Christ,
shall bring us safely to a birth.

So then in this season of abandonment,
teach us abandonment.
May we burn the words we worship
and release the things we revere.
May we be made virginal,
a place for the Babe to be born.

Amen

Prayer for Renewal

O Beloved Spirit,
In this winter time,
when the media tells us what we believe we are,
and captions what we believe we know,
nurture what is green, Evergreen.

In this winter time,
when what we hear has been said
in so many scriptures and poems and plays
that we can no longer hear it,
nurture what is green, Evergreen.

In this winter time,
when our desire for more is only in what we own
and our desire to become is only in what we do,
nurture what is green, Evergreen.

In this winter time,
when darkness shortens our hold on the light
and the days are dwarfed by our increasing need to want,
nurture what is green, Evergreen.

In this winter time,
when we have grown so afraid of injustice
that we have no impetus to be just,
when we have grown so afraid of pain
that we have no will to risk the pain of growing,
when we have grown so afraid of what others may think
that we have no power to think thoughts sacred and singular,
nurture what is green, Evergreen.

In this winter time,
renew the birth, rekindle the waning fire.
Amid all our gadgets and libraries of words
and museums of memories and jaded observations,
nurture what is green, Evergreen.

Amen

Prayer in Anticipation

O Beloved Spirit,
We are graced in this time of encroaching darkness
with the anticipation of an arrival:
a birth of spirit,
a renewal of expanding light,
a reunion of intersecting love.

We are graced in this time of encroaching darkness
with the charged excitement of gifts to be given:
blessings to bloom,
surprises to delight,
openings to reveal.

We are graced in this time of encroaching darkness
with the advent of a timeless return:
pregnant with hope,
seamed with longing,
awake with anticipation.

In this Advent season that is
mixed into the adventure of being Human,
we give homage to the generative lights
of those who have inspired us,
who have awakened in us new birth,
new breakthroughs,
new transformations.

In this Advent season that is
mixed into the adventure of being Human,
we carry into the ever darkening day,
the love You have planted in our hearts,
the love that connects us as one body,
the love that lights up our days
with hope and anticipation.

Amen

Prayer for Renewal of Light

O Beloved Spirit,
We've lost anchor
and have no hold.
The darkness folds in
upon the light
and bounds our days
with the uncertain.

We seem left with less
and full of loss,
at a time when we need
so much of more.

And while we know
all the places that it is not,
we carry the worry
that that's all we can ever know.
Time squeezes us tighter toward
shortened margins of light.

This Advent, must it be
one toward ever-darkening days
or is there birth in its midst?

Dispel our fear.
Embolden our hope.
Deepen our love
that we might realign our days
to the birth in this season;
to the renewal of light in our hearts.

Amen

Prayer for New Immanuel

O Beloved Spirit,
Huge encroachments of darkness
blot each end of the day
and compress the light into less and less space.
There is so little room left,
no expansion, no birth, no openings.
Where is our Immanuel?

Huge encroachments of darkness, like a vise,
squeeze out all the potential
leaving us owning only the urgent.
No time to pray, to contemplate, to laugh.
Where is our Immanuel?

Huge encroachments of darkness
no longer just sit on either end of the day
but now their dark starts to close
what could have been our openings.
The cares, the concerns, the expectations,
the unknowns, the fears,
like blinders, cut short our wider vision, our higher vision.
We see only the most immediate.
Having lost sight of the most important,
where is our Immanuel?

This is our winter season.
It is blanketed in the cold, stripped, barren landscape
where even our sleep is devoid of dreams.
O Beloved Spirit, reawaken the ground of us.
Stir and quicken new life in us.
Let the baby be born in the manger
of our work and our constrictions.
Let the Immanuel we seek without
be the Immanuel reborn within.
Let Christmas find its birth in us.

Amen

Prayer to the Brink of Our Birth

O Beloved Spirit,
It seems the millenniums have worked their way
to this time and this place and brought us to a stable with a manger.
It seems so many universes have bloomed into dark matter and
galaxies of stars bringing us to this one bright star ablaze overhead.
It seems so many ancestors have brought into play our eye color, our
height, our disposition and brought us here
to this brink of our birth.

Though You have sealed us from our before and our hereafter,
You have swaddled us in time with the immense *potentia* of Now.
Though You've hidden from us the inner-workings of this Moment,
You have gifted us with a legacy of music, poetry, scriptures.
Though You have limited us with a begin date and an end date,
You bounded our finite days
with graced access to the Infinite, the Holy, the Marvelous.

Though we feel at times we have come up short,
short-changed this chance to be, somehow sold ourselves short,
You have infused our lives with love and forgiveness.
Though we feel there is too much to achieve,
too much to know, so much unknowable,
You deepen our days with *kairos* and let us restore in the timeless,
in the holding of babies, in the intense conversations of prayer.
Though we feel there is not enough time, not enough mercy,
not enough imagination to rescue us from our darker selves,
You enthuse our very being
with an inexplicable joy that gets us through.

As we process with the ever-shortening of the days
and feel the press of the encroaching darkness,
let us remember that we are on the brink of our birth,
that there is the potential to be and become a bloom of light,
as our star is the world's chance to be,
as our birth is the world's chance to see the Christ born within us,
as our manifestation of You is the world's chance to Go in Love.
Let us embrace this Advent,
Let us embrace this brink of our birth.

Amen

Prayer at Christmas

O Beloved Spirit,
The gift of birth is all around us
and inside us.
So much life waiting to be named
and unfold through us and around us.
Accept our gratefulness for the birth and rebirth
renewed in the season of the Christ born in a manger.

Accept our gratefulness
for the riches You have bestowed on us—
in the loves we know,
in the friendships we cultivate,
in the amazing miracle of life and renewed life.

Amen

Prayer for the Epiphany

O Beloved Spirit,
More personal than all the things we desire,
more unique than the opinions we have acquired,
more vital than the talents we can display,
the epiphany of You in us.

As if You are the breath that sounds out
and through the song we sing,
as if You are the intoxicant
that sets us trilling with joy,
as if You are the longing for life
beyond the death we must conceive,
the epiphany of You in us.

Star above,
whose light illuminates
the manger of our work, our deeds, our desires,
shine over us in a shout of light
and call out in us the recognition:
there is a child of God-given birth this day,
the epiphany of You in us.

Amen

Prayer to the Christ Born Within Us

O Beloved Spirit,
O Holy Christ born within us,
Be like a blessing and not a curse of untapped potential.
Be like a bloom and not a thorn of inadequacies.
Be like a star and not an anchor of times lost.
Be like a song and not a list of things undone.
Be like a dance and not a clock carving time into pieces.

O Holy Christ born within us, be like a full-bodied bread
of daily sustenance that goes down good,
awakening our senses to a heightened experience of being alive,
nourishing all our centers of heart, mind and passion
moving us to act, to create, to initiate,
to pray in an outburst of Holy, Holy, Holy.

O Holy Christ born within us, be like a beneficent chalice of grace
from which we drink deeply, from which we articulate widely;
that intoxicates us with a joy,
that moves us into color and into poetry and into song,
into rhythm, into movement and transubstantiates us into a
spontaneous "Ahhhhh" and "OMMMM" and "Ohhhh"
and escapes on our breath like a blessing.

O Holy Christ born within us, may we go
like a blessing, like a bloom, like a star,
like a song, like a dance
and may we go in love, be bathed in love, be fully immersed in love
and know You fully as the body and blood of sweet communion—
to know You as the bread and the chalice of our daily intercourse,
to know You as the nourishment, a taste of immortality,
and the grace of the moment now robed in Always.

May we go like a blessing,
like a bloom, like a star,
like a song, like a dance.
May we go in love.

Amen

Prayer to Belove

O Beloved Spirit,
It strikes us how many hidden streams river through us
and how unaware we are of what profound experiences
animate the lives of those we know by name.
It strikes us how connected we are through the unseen;
and yet, how far apart we seem when measuring our differences.
It strikes us how uniquely crafted we are with our sequencing of DNA
and yet, how seamed together we are through
the collective awakenings to Your Holy Spirit.
Too much of the time, we are kept at bay
by the unfathomable cliché of being One,
unable to penetrate to an epiphany of You in Each, in All of Us.

O Beloved Spirit, be love in us.
Be love through us.
Belove us, belove us, belove us.

We are not broken in truth but broken in our perception.
We are not fragmented in fact but fragmented in our action.
Be love in us.
Be love through us.
Belove us, belove us, belove us.

How far away we can become from the Where-we-are,
from the Who-we-are, from the Community we are becoming.
Reunite us with the beloving that calls us to our star,
that calls us to the universe's one chance to be,
that calls us to bear the bloom of love, the fruit of light.
Be love in us.
Be love through us.
Belove us, belove us, belove us.

Amen